Everyday Things

Childcraft

1992 Childcraft Annual — a **Childcraft** title
Childcraft Reg. US Pat. Off. Marca Registrada

Published by World Book International
525 West Monroe Street
Chicago, Illinois 60661
USA

Printed in USA.

ISBN 0-7166-6192-6

A/IB

Childcraft Annual

Everyday
Things

World Book International
a World Book Company
Chicago London Sydney

Contents

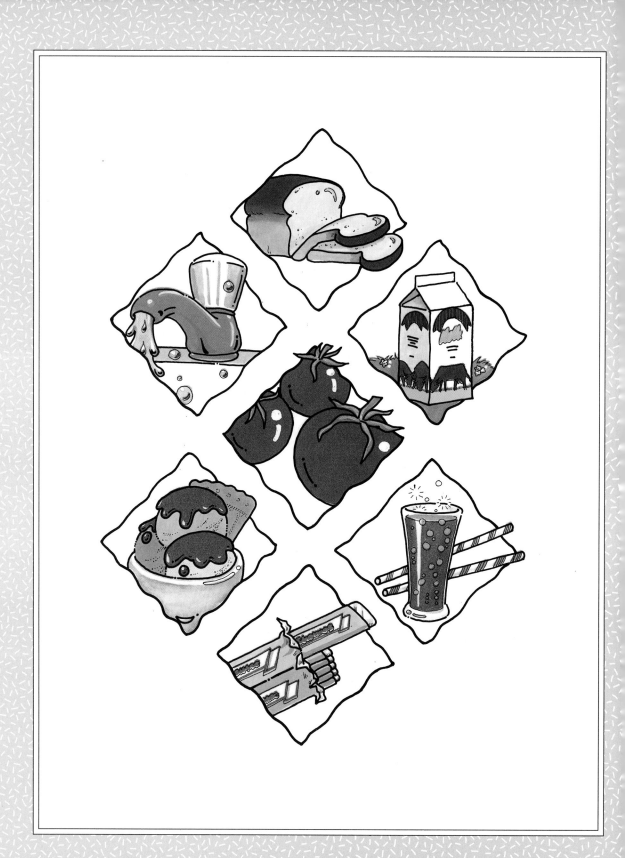

FIND OUT ABOUT

things you eat and drink

How is bread made?
What puts the fizz in lemonade?
Where does chewing gum come from?

The bread machine

Maybe you remember the story of Little Red Hen, who couldn't get her lazy friends to help her to make bread. Here's a new version. This time, Little Red Hen doesn't make the bread herself. She uses machines to help her and the job gets done much more easily.

Bread comes from a plant called wheat. Once the wheat in the field has grown tall and golden, it is time to harvest it. Do you remember how in the story Little Red Hen said, "The wheat is ripe now. Who will help me cut it?" And do you remember the replies?

"Not I," said the duck.
"Not I," said the cat.
"Not I," said the dog.

This is how the new version of the story goes.

"Very well," said Little Red Hen. "I will use a machine called a combine harvester to cut the wheat. The combine harvester will remove the ears of grain at the top of the stalk. It will also strip off the covering, called the husk, from each grain. Then it will pour the grain into my truck."

When the truck was full of wheat grain, Little Red Hen asked, "Now, who's ready to help me grind the wheat into flour?"

"Not I," said the duck.

"Not I," said the cat.

"Not I," said the dog.

"I should have known," replied Little Red Hen. "Very well. I will take my wheat to a flour mill."

Not I!

FLOUR MILL

At the mill, Little Red Hen's wheat was tipped into a big grinder. The grain was ground between huge rollers and then sifted until it became a fine flour. In another machine the flour was poured into bags, which were then sealed shut. Little Red Hen left the mill with a truck full of flour bags.

"Who's ready to help me make bread out of my flour?" she asked.

"Not I," said the duck.

"Not I," said the cat.

"Not I," said the dog.

"I just thought I'd ask," said Little Red Hen. "Very well. I will take my flour to the bakery."

Bread words

yeast
A spoonful of yeast contains thousands of tiny plants. These feed on the sugar in bread dough. When they take in this sugary food, they increase in number. Soon there are thousands more particles of yeast.

As they grow, they make a gas called carbon dioxide. This gas makes the small bubbles in the dough which help to make the bread rise. Yeast can only feed on the sugar when it's kept in a warm place.

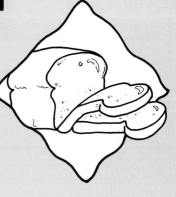

At the bakery, a machine mixed the flour with yeast, water, salt, oil and a little sugar until it became a sticky dough. The dough sat in a tank in a warm room until the yeast made tiny bubbles in the dough. The dough rose to double its size.

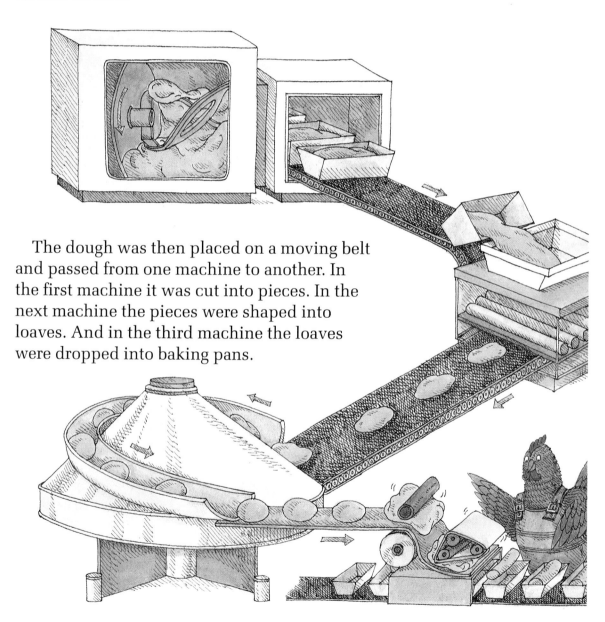

The dough was then placed on a moving belt and passed from one machine to another. In the first machine it was cut into pieces. In the next machine the pieces were shaped into loaves. And in the third machine the loaves were dropped into baking pans.

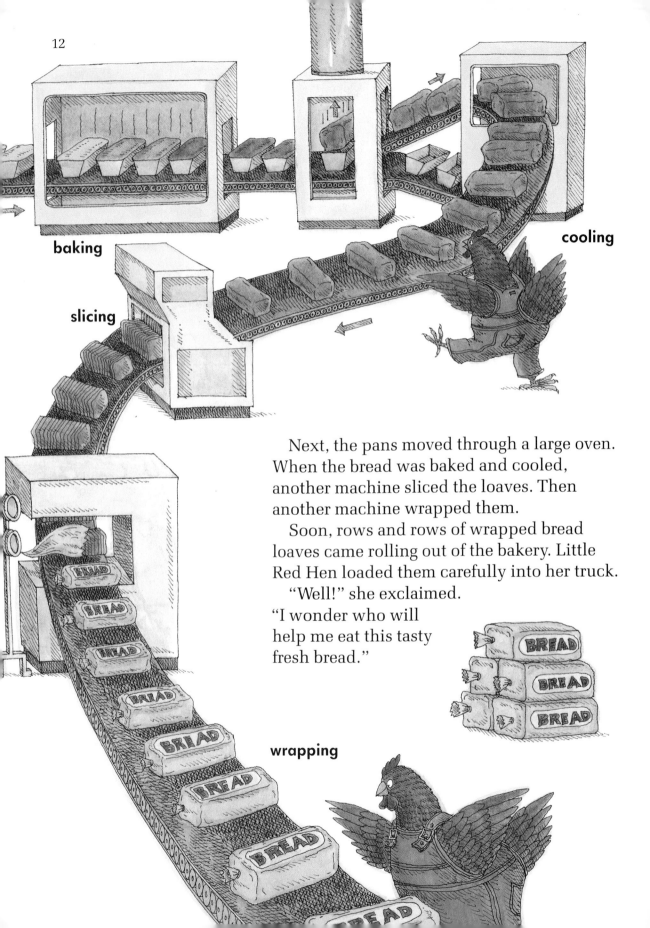

12

baking

cooling

slicing

Next, the pans moved through a large oven.
When the bread was baked and cooled,
another machine sliced the loaves. Then
another machine wrapped them.

Soon, rows and rows of wrapped bread
loaves came rolling out of the bakery. Little
Red Hen loaded them carefully into her truck.

"Well!" she exclaimed.
"I wonder who will
help me eat this tasty
fresh bread."

BREAD
BREAD
BREAD

wrapping

"I will!" said the duck.

"I will!" said the cat.

"I will!" said the dog.

"Not so fast!" said Little Red Hen. "I don't remember getting any help from any of you when I asked. If you want to eat my tasty bread, you will have to buy it."

"I don't mind so much that my friends didn't help me make bread," she said to herself. "The combine harvester, the mill and the bakery made the job much easier, anyway."

FUN TO DO

Little Red Hen made bread out of wheat. How would you like to make a bread hen?

14

FUN TO DO

Little bread hen

1. Take the crusts off the bread and break it into tiny crumbs in the bowl.

2. Add the 6 teaspoons of white glue, liquid detergent and food colouring. Stir the mixture.

3. Now roll the dough with your hands until it becomes a smooth ball.

YOU WILL NEED:

6 slices of soft white
   bread
6 teaspoons of white
   glue
½ teaspoon of liquid
   detergent
few drops of red food
   colouring
a bowl
a spoon
paper and a pencil
small scissors
wax paper
a rolling pin
a blunt knife
a toothpick
1 tablespoon of glue
1 tablespoon of water
a paint brush
varnish

* Ask your parents to
help you.

4. Put the paper over the picture of Little Red Hen shown here. Trace the hen's outline onto the paper and cut it out.

Remember!
Your dough hen is a model.
It is not for eating!

5. On the wax paper, roll the dough out flat. It should be about as thick as one of your fingers.

6. Stick your picture of Little Red Hen onto the dough. Using the picture as a guide, cut out a hen from the dough using a pair of scissors or a blunt knife.

7. Use the toothpick to carve Little Red Hen's eye and wing.

8. Mix together the glue and the water. With the brush, paint this glue mixture onto the hen. This will keep the dough from cracking as it dries.

9. Leave your dough hen on the wax paper in a cool, dry place for about 12 hours.

10. If you want your hen to last a long time, ask an adult to help you coat it with varnish when it is dry.

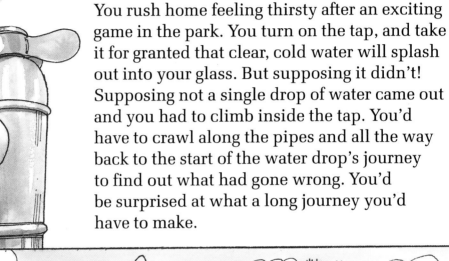

FOOD AND DRINK

A water drop's journey

You rush home feeling thirsty after an exciting game in the park. You turn on the tap, and take it for granted that clear, cold water will splash out into your glass. But supposing it didn't! Supposing not a single drop of water came out and you had to climb inside the tap. You'd have to crawl along the pipes and all the way back to the start of the water drop's journey to find out what had gone wrong. You'd be surprised at what a long journey you'd have to make.

reservoir

Water comes from underground, and also from rivers, lakes and streams. Water from all these places can be drained off and stored in an artificial lake called a reservoir. Reservoirs are often built near towns and cities, where people use huge amounts of water every day. But the water in reservoirs contains dirt and germs which make it dangerous to drink. So the water drop must travel on from the reservoir to a water treatment works to be cleaned before it arrives at your tap.

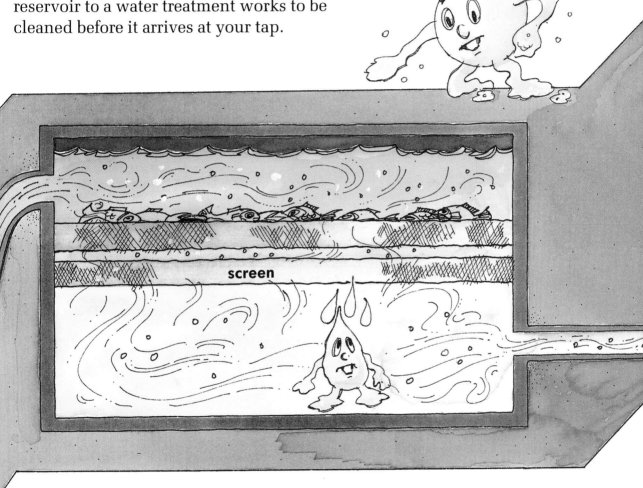

screen

At the water treatment works, the water drop first goes through a screen. The screen stops dead fish, leaves and other large things from passing through with the water.

Next, the water drop flows into a mixing basin. Here, chemicals are poured into the water to make it safe to drink. One of the chemicals is called alum. Particles of dirt in the water stick to the alum. Small amounts of a gas called chlorine are also added to kill any germs in the water.

alum

chlorine

mixing basin

settling basin

From the mixing basin, the water drop moves to the settling basin. Here the dirt falls to the bottom, or settles. The water drop leaves the settling basin and passes through filters which remove any tiny particles of dirt that are left. The filters are made of layers of charcoal, sand and gravel. More chlorine is added to the water.

Another chemical called fluoride may also be added. This helps to keep your teeth strong.

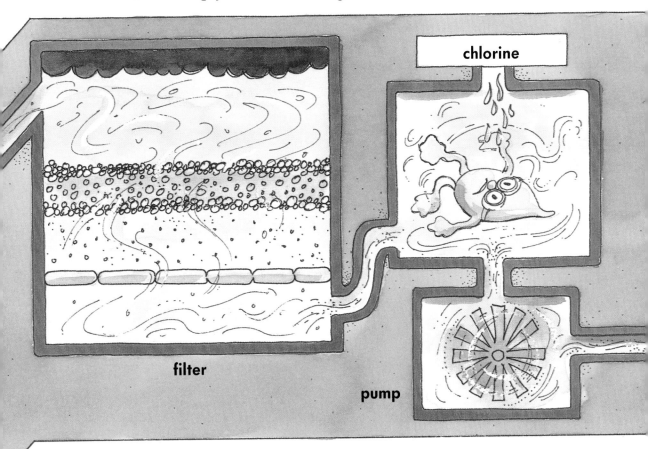

filter

pump

chlorine

Water words

fluoride
Fluoride is a chemical which comes from a mineral called fluorspar. Fluoride greatly reduces tooth decay, so it is added to toothpaste as well as to water.

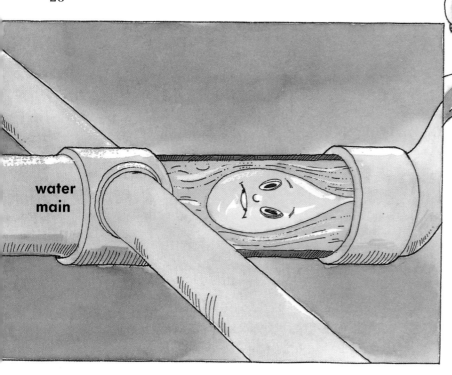

water main

The water drop is finally ready to leave the water treatment works on the last part of its journey. It is pumped out of the works into big pipes under the streets, called water mains. Water flows through the mains to pipes that go right into your house. Then you turn on the tap and the water drop falls into your glass — with lots of others, of course!

FUN TO DO

You can see how water is cleaned by making your own filter.

FUN TO DO

A water filter

YOU WILL NEED:

an empty plastic
    bottle
scissors
cotton wool
muddy water
small, clean pebbles
clean gravel
clean sand

* **Ask your parents to
help you.**

1. Cut off the top of the plastic bottle with your scissors, about 8-10 centimetres down from the lid. Turn the top upside down and rest it in the bottom half of the bottle.

2. Push a ball of cotton wool into the neck of the bottle. Put in a layer of small pebbles, then one of gravel, then one of wet sand.

3. Pour some muddy water onto the sand and watch it drip through into the bottom of the bottle. You'll see that the water now looks cleaner.

**Remember!
Don't drink your filtered
water — it might still
have germs in it.**

The story of milk

Milk is not only a delicious drink, it is also the main part of many of our favourite foods. Think of milk shakes and ice-cream, milk chocolate, yoghurt and cheese. None of these would exist without milk. We get milk from cows, goats, sheep and other animals. Animals like these are called mammals. They make milk inside their bodies to feed their young. This is called lactation.

In many countries, cows are kept on dairy farms to provide milk for people. The cows must be milked every day. Most cows are now milked by machine because it is faster and cleaner than milking by hand.

The milking machine has special cups which fit onto the cow's udders. The cups gently squeeze the teats, just like a calf sucking. The milk flows into a jar.

Milk words

Pasteurization

Pasteurization is a process that is named after the French scientist who discovered it, Louis Pasteur. Pasteur found that diseases are spread by germs. Germs make people ill. Pasteur found that if you heat food to a certain temperature for the right length of time, the germs are killed.

The milk is warm when it comes out of the cow, which means that germs can start growing in it. To stop this from happening, the milk is cooled in a big tank. Next, the milk is pumped into a tank on a truck. The truck takes the milk from the dairy farm to a processing plant.

At the processing plant, some or all of the thick, fatty part of the milk, called the cream, may be taken out of the milk by machine. The cream can be sold by itself or made into other food such as butter or ice-cream.

The amount of cream, or fat, left in the milk is measured, and other tests are made to check that the milk is of good quality. The milk now has to be heated to kill off any other harmful germs. This is called pasteurization. Next the milk is homogenized. This means that the milk is mixed up so that the fat that is left does not rise in a layer to the top.

Lastly, the milk is poured by a machine into cartons or bottles. The cartons and bottles are sealed. Trucks take the milk straight to the shops so that we can buy it fresh every day.

FUN TO DO

Find out how to make your own butter.

FUN TO DO ▶ Butter

YOU WILL NEED:

¼ **litre of thick cream**
a bowl
a mixer
a wire strainer
1 litre of iced water
¼ **teaspoon of salt**
a spoon

1. Leave the cream out of the refrigerator for about an hour. Cream will become butter faster if it is not too cold.

2. Pour the cream into the bowl. Start beating it. You'll need to keep beating for a long time! Little globs of fat will form in the bowl after about 5 minutes. This is your butter.

3. There will be some liquid left over after the butter forms. This is called buttermilk. You can drain off the buttermilk and drink it later.

4. Scrape the butter from the bowl. Put it in the wire strainer. Hold the strainer over a sink. Slowly pour the iced water over the butter to wash it.

5. Put the butter back in the bowl. With a spoon, mix in the salt. Now you can spread your home-made butter on hot toast and eat it!

* Ask your parents to help you.

FOOD
AND
DRINK

Who invented cheese?

There is a legend about how an Arab traveller accidentally made the first cheese.

One day, over 4,000 years ago, an Arab traveller — let's call him Hasan — made a trip across the desert. Hasan took some milk with him to drink on the way. He stored his milk in a pouch made from a sheep's stomach.

At the end of the long, hot day Hasan was thirsty. He opened his pouch to drink the milk. But it smelled sour and looked watery and lumpy. Hasan was really hungry, so he ate one of the lumps. He was surprised to find that it tasted delicious — it was cheese!

So what happened to Hasan's milk? Inside the stomach of some animals like sheep, there is a chemical known as rennin. The milk had been churned with the rennin in the sheep's warm stomach and had thickened. Soft lumps called curds and a thin liquid called whey formed. It is the curd part of the mixture that makes cheese.

This may not really be how people first found out about cheese! But cheese is still made in much the same way in factories today.

How cheese is made

Cheese-makers pour milk into large tanks. They warm the milk and then add a special liquid known as a starter to the milk. The starter contains tiny living things called bacteria, which turn the milk sour. Next they add rennin to separate the milk into curds and whey.

The curds are heated until they are firm, then the whey is drained off. The curds are squeezed to remove more whey. Machines cut the curd and press it into metal moulds. Next, the curd is salted and the moulds are moved to a warm room. The cheese has to be left in this room until it has just the right flavour. We call this process ageing. Some kinds of cheese must age for many months.

The room where the cheese is aged is called a ripening room. The room is kept at a constant temperature.

Cheese words

Bacteria

Bacteria are tiny living organisms in the air, water and soil, and even inside other living beings. You can only see them through a microscope. Some bacteria are harmful and may cause disease. Most bacteria won't hurt you, though. In fact, some bacteria help us, such as the bacteria used to make cheese.

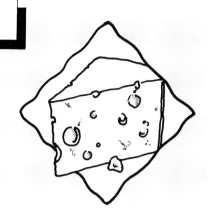

What makes the holes in Swiss cheese?

Have you ever seen that special type of cheese with holes in it? We call it Swiss cheese, because most of it is made in Switzerland. This kind of cheese has been made for over 500 years and because Swiss cheese needs such a lot of care to make, cheese-makers often call it the 'king of the cheeses'. How do you think the holes get into Swiss cheese?

Special bacteria are added to the curd. When the temperature is just right, the bacteria give off bubbles of a gas called carbon dioxide. As the cheese ages and hardens, the bubbles, called eyes, get bigger. They are like large air pockets in the cheese and they take a few weeks to form. When you slice the cheese, you can see the holes inside.

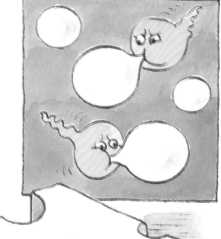

The tale of the tomato

One day in 1820, a crowd gathered at the steps of a courthouse in New Jersey in the United States of America. They were watching a man called Colonel Robert Gibbon Johnson eating tomatoes. This seems quite an ordinary thing to us, but in New Jersey in 1820 it was an amazing event. In those days, many people believed that it was dangerous to eat tomatoes because the tomato plant belongs to a family of poisonous plants. Everyone stared as Colonel Johnson ate tomato after tomato.

"He's crazy!" said one person. "He'll die!"

To the surprise of the onlookers, when Colonel Johnson finished eating, he was alive and well. He knew that tomatoes are good to eat. After that day, word spread quickly through North America and more and more people began to eat tomatoes.

Tomato words

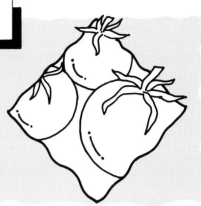

ketchup
The first ketchups had no tomato in them at all. The name 'ketchup' comes from the Chinese word 'ke-tsiap'. Ke-tsiap is a sauce made from pickled fish and spices. Many thick, spicy sauces used to be called ketchup. Today, tomato ketchup is probably the best-known sauce in the world!

Tomatoes originally came from South America. The wild tomato is a red berry about the size of a grape. It has a stronger, sweeter flavour than the tomato we know. We eat tomatoes as a vegetable. But did you know that they are really a fruit? Perhaps that's one reason why they were also known as love apples. Another reason is that people who ate them were supposed to fall in love!

Today, we eat tomatoes all the time. We eat raw tomatoes, canned tomatoes, tomato juice, tomato soup, tomato sauce, ketchup... There are so many ways to eat tomatoes. What's your favourite way?

The big scoop!

Quick! Lick up that trickle of ice-cream before it runs down the cone and on to your hand! Everyone loves to eat a big scoop of ice-cream on a hot day. As you can tell from its name, ice-cream is made from frozen cream. Sugar, water and flavouring are also added. Ice-cream is made in a special way so that it is smooth and delicious.

The cream, sugar and water are mixed together in large tanks, or vats, at the ice-cream factory. When the mixture is smooth and cool, the flavour is added. Then the ice-cream is frozen in huge freezers.

As the ice-cream freezes, special knives inside the freezer whip the mixture, adding air. The air softens the ice-cream. If no air was added, the ice-cream would be too hard to scoop and eating it would be like eating frozen ice cubes!

There are so many different flavours of ice-cream. What's your favourite flavour? Is it chocolate, toffee, mint or maybe vanilla? Where do these delicious tastes come from? The answer is that many of the flavours are artificial. This means that they are made from chemicals and not from fruit or plant juices. These artificial flavours are made in a laboratory by scientists.

Scientists called flavourists can match natural flavours by mixing the right chemicals together. But some flavours are too difficult for even the most clever flavourist to match. So some ice-cream is best flavoured with natural flavours.

Ice-cream words

flavour

There are four basic types of flavour: sweet, salty, sour and bitter. You can tell what flavour you are eating because of special cells on your tongue and the roof of your mouth called taste buds. The smell of a food also helps you to decide what flavour it is.

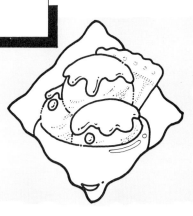

cacao
tree

cacao
pod

cacao
beans

cocoa
butter

cocoa
powder

Bean-flavoured ice-cream?

Chocolate and vanilla may be two of your favourite ice-cream flavours. Did you know that they are made from beans? Chocolate is made from the beans of the tropical cacao tree. Seed pods about the size of a coconut grow on the tree. Each pod contains from 20 to 50 cream-coloured beans. When the beans are taken out of the pod, they are left out in the air. After a few days, they turn brown and have a chocolate taste.

At the chocolate factory, cacao beans are cleaned, roasted and shelled. Next, the shelled beans, or nibs, are ground between heavy stone or steel wheels. The heat from the grinding melts the nibs and a thick, dark chocolate liquid is made.

Then the liquid is pressed until it separates into yellow cocoa butter and a light brown cake. The cake is ground into cocoa powder. This is what the makers of ice-cream use to flavour chocolate ice-cream. Scientists still can't find a recipe for a really good artificial chocolate.

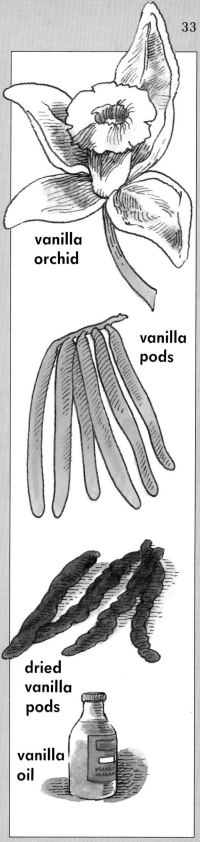

vanilla
orchid

vanilla
pods

dried
vanilla
pods

vanilla
oil

Vanilla flavour can be made from chemicals. It is called vanillin. But natural vanilla comes from beans, too. The beans are called pods and they grow on a flower called an orchid. Vanilla pods are long and green and must be dried before they can be used. Drying, or curing, the pods usually takes about six months.

During this time, the pods shrink and turn dark brown. Now they are coated with vanilla oil. The cured pods are crushed to take out the oil which is used to flavour vanilla ice-cream. Natural vanilla is an expensive flavour because it takes a long time to make.

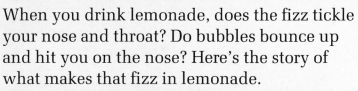

FOOD AND DRINK

Where does lemonade get its fizz?

When you drink lemonade, does the fizz tickle your nose and throat? Do bubbles bounce up and hit you on the nose? Here's the story of what makes that fizz in lemonade.

In some places, fizzy water comes bubbling straight out of the ground. Many years ago, people thought that this water had special powers. They believed that if they drank it or bathed in it, they might be cured of certain illnesses.

The demand for this water was so great that scientists tried making it. In 1772, the English chemist, Joseph Priestley, succeeded. He dissolved carbon dioxide in water. Carbon dioxide is the gas that makes the spring water bubble from the ground. The result of Joseph Priestley's experiment was a new kind of water which we call carbonated water.

Soon, this carbonated water was being bottled. Chemists sold it as medicine. They added leaves from different plants to increase the water's healing powers. This also gave the water a pleasant taste. By the end of the 1800s, chemists were making many different flavours. Fizzy drinks are still made from carbonated water today. But today, drinks like lemonade are made in factories, not by chemists.

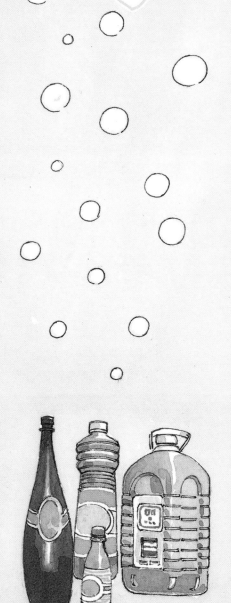

Lemonade words

baking powder

Baking powder is a fine, white powder. It contains starch, bicarbonate of soda and acid-forming ingredients. The bicarbonate of soda reacts with the acid, when liquid is added, to make carbon dioxide gas. Baking powder is also added to the mixture for cakes and biscuits. The carbon dioxide makes the mixture rise so that the cakes and biscuits are light.

Has anyone ever asked you if you want a glass of soda pop when they mean a glass of fizzy drink? Do you know why they call it soda pop? Scientists used bicarbonate of soda, which is also called baking powder, to add carbon dioxide to water. So people started calling carbonated water soda. The name pop came about because bottles of carbonated water were sealed with corks. When the bottles were opened, the corks made a popping sound.

POP

FUN TO DO

You can use baking soda to make a delicious fizzy drink.

Orange fizz

FUN TO DO

YOU WILL NEED:

a medium-sized
   drinking glass
orange juice
½ teaspoon of baking
   powder
a spoon

* **Ask your parents to help you.**

1. Fill the glass about one-half to two-thirds full with orange juice.

2. Add the baking powder and stir gently.

3. Watch as the bubbles rise.

4. Sip your drink. Does it taste just like fizzy orangeade?

**FOOD
AND
DRINK**

The story of chewing gum

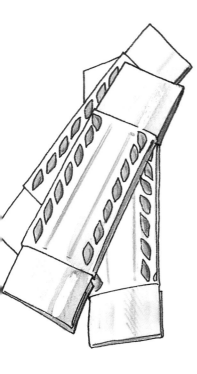

1. Collecting the chicle
2. Boiling the chicle
3. Moulding chicle into slabs
4. Transporting the chicle

Do you like chewing gum? Do you chew it for hours and hours until there's no flavour left at all? While your teeth are working away, you might find you can concentrate better. Or you might just end up with an aching jaw! Did you know that people have been chewing gum-like substances for hundreds of years? These gums came from sticky liquids that formed on the bark of trees.

Chewing gum is made from a milky gum which comes from a tropical tree called the sapodilla tree. The juice is called chicle and it flows out of the tree when the bark is cut. Workers in the tropical rain forests use long knives to cut zig-zag grooves in the trunk of the sapodilla tree. The chicle flows slowly down into a bucket at the foot of the tree. Long ago, people could take the gum straight from the tree. Today, chewing gum still comes from a tree, but it has to go through a long process before it reaches us.

The workers have to boil the chicle to remove most of the water from it. The chicle is then moulded into big slabs weighing between 9 and 14 kilograms. Mules or canoes carry the slabs through the jungle to planes at nearby airstrips. The planes take the chicle to ships that sail to other parts of the world where the chewing gum will be made in factories.

Chewing gum words

foil
Foil is made of extremely thin sheets of a metal called aluminium. The aluminium is beaten and rolled until it is as thin as a leaf. Foil is often used as a wrapping for food. It keeps food fresh. The foil used to wrap all the chewing gum made each year would make a strip almost half a metre wide stretching from the Earth to the Moon!

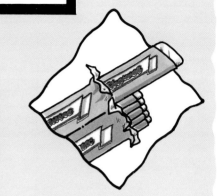

At the chewing gum factory, the chicle is placed in large kettles along with other artificial gums. These ingredients are heated up to make the chewing gum base. Powdered sugar and flavours are added.

Machines mix the gum slowly until it looks like a stiff bread dough. Then it is pressed into a wide sheet and sent to the sheet rolling machine. These rollers work just like rolling pins! They flatten the gum into a thin, wide ribbon. Next, machines divide the gum into smaller sheets and mark where the sticks will be cut. Other machines break these sheets into single sticks. More powdered sugar may be sprinkled on the sticks to stop them sticking together.

One machine with over 6,000 working parts wraps the sticks of gum in foil and paper, and seals them in a package. The wrappers keep the chewing gum fresh until you unwrap it!

1. Heating the chicle
2. Adding sugar and flavour
3. Rolling the gum
4. Wrapping the sticks

FIND OUT ABOUT

things
you wear

Where does cotton come from?
Can cloth be made from oil?
Who made the first sports shoes?

From sheep to sweater

When do you wear what a sheep once wore? When you wear a wool sweater, of course! Most woollen clothes are made from a sheep's coat, which we call a fleece.

Thousands of years ago, people discovered that wool from sheep can be made into yarn. They found that the yarn made comfortable clothes which could keep them warm and dry.

Today, we still take wool from sheep and turn it into clothes. And the way we do this is very similar to the way people used to make all their own clothes. Machines just make the process faster.

This Australian sheep shearer is using electric clippers to shear a sheep.

Once a year, usually when the weather is growing warmer, sheep have their fleece cut off. We call this shearing. Shearing used to be done by hand, but now most shearing is done by machine. Expert sheep shearers cut the fleece off in one piece and they can shear up to 200 sheep in one day.

The cut fleeces are sent to a factory called a scouring plant. Here, the wool is washed to remove the dirt and most of the grease. Then it is combed, or carded, into thin threads to take out any knots. The threads of wool, called fibres, are untangled and spread apart into soft, loose strands.

Wool words

fibre
A fibre is a long strand of any substance, such as cotton or wool. It can be at least 100 times longer than it is wide. Fibres can be spun into yarn and made into fabric.

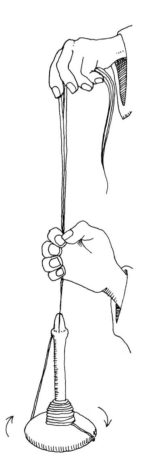

Next comes the spinning. The loose threads are twisted and pulled at the same time. The earliest spinners spun the fibres by hand. They took the wool in one hand and drew it out, twisting it into a thread with the fingers of the other hand. The first wooden spinning wheels were made in India about 1,500 years ago. For a long time, wool was spun on a wheel throughout the world. Today, most wool is spun by machine. Spinning machines twist each thread into yarn.

Most sheep's wool is a shade of creamy-white when it is cut from the sheep's back. But we want our clothes to be all kinds of colours. So we use dyes to make the wool the colour we want. In the past, people used flowers, leaves and other natural materials to make dyes. Today, dyes are usually made from chemicals.

Once the wool is dyed, it can be turned into clothes. Making clothes from one length of woollen yarn is called knitting. In hand knitting, you use two smooth rods called needles to make loops of yarn. The loops join together to make one piece of fabric. Because of the loops, knitted clothes stretch easily.

Woollen yarn can also be woven into cloth. Weaving uses two or more lengths of yarn, called the warp. The warp threads are stretched in one direction across a frame, or loom. Then another piece of yarn, called the weft, is used. The weft moves over and under the warp threads, back and forth.

If you have a sweater, it is probably a knitted one. Woven wool is usually used for thick clothes like coats. Next time you wear any kind of woollen clothes, think of the sheep who first wore the wool!

knitting

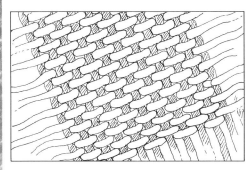

weaving

FUN TO DO

You don't need a large loom to do some weaving. You can make a loom out of card.

FUN TO DO

A woven mat

YOU WILL NEED:

a piece of thick card,
    20 centimetres square
a ruler
a pencil
scissors
a large darning
    needle
wool of different
    colours
adhesive tape
a fork or a comb

* Ask your parents to
help you.

1. First, you need to make a loom from card. Draw two lines on the card, one centimetre from the top and bottom edges. Mark off points half a centimetre apart along each line.

2. Cut down and along between every other mark to make a notch. The top and bottom of your loom should look like rows of teeth.

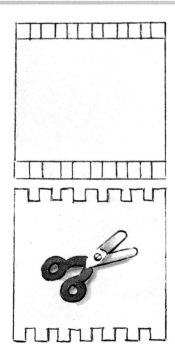

3. Now you are ready to wind on the row of warp threads. Fasten one end of a piece of wool to the back of the card with adhesive tape. Loop the wool backwards and forwards round the notches, keeping it as tight as you can. When the whole of one side is covered, cut the wool and tape the other end to the back of the card.

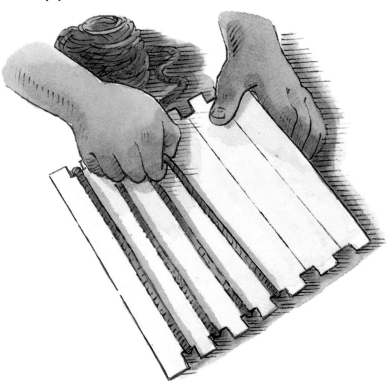

Remember!
Be careful when you're using
the sharp needle.

4. You can now begin weaving in the weft. Thread the needle with wool of another colour. Starting at the base of the loom, weave the wool in and out of the warp threads, going under and over. When you reach the other side, go back again, this time weaving over and under the warp.

5. Carry on weaving, one row over and under, the next under and over. With the fork or comb, push the weft down every few minutes towards the bottom of the loom. This makes the rows even.

6. Change colour whenever you like. To finish one colour, leave a tail of wool hanging at the back of the weaving. Start a new colour from the back in the same way. The loose threads can be tied together later.

7. When the weaving is finished, carefully unhook the loops from the card notches. Knot the loose ends together and tuck them into the weaving.

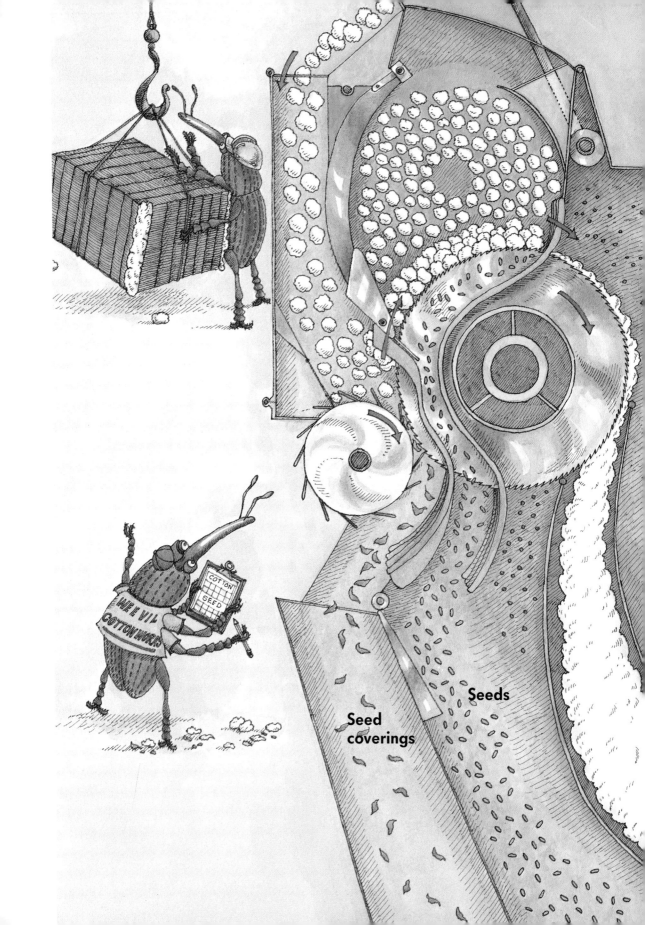

Seeds

Seed
coverings

From cotton to T-shirt

Cotton is one of the most useful fabrics we have. Look around you. How many things made of cotton can you see? What about your clothes? Then there are towels, and don't forget sheets. Lots of things are made of cotton because it is a strong, comfortable fabric and because it is easy to wash. But what is cotton, and how does it get made into things like T-shirts?

Cotton is a soft, white ball of fibres. It comes from the seed pod, or boll, of the cotton plant. Each boll contains about 30 seeds. Fibres of cotton grow from each of the seeds. A cotton fibre takes about three weeks to grow and one ripe boll can contain up to 500,000 fibres of cotton. Picking machines pluck the cotton from each ripe boll.

The carding machine combs the fibres until they are straight.

This machine is called a ring spinner. It twists the yarn and winds it onto spools, or bobbins, at the bottom.

The picked cotton is sent through a machine called a cotton gin. The gin separates the fibres from the seeds. Next, the cotton is pressed into big slabs called bales, so that it is easy to send to other factories.

The cotton will be made into lengths of material at a textile factory. The cotton is first cleaned and broken up into smaller pieces. It is then spread on to a carding machine. The carding machine uses huge rollers covered with wire teeth to make the fibres stronger and straighter.

At this stage, the cotton fibres are spun on spinning machines, which twist and pull the

This loom can weave several different colours of warp and weft. The woven cloth is wound up on a roller at the front of the loom.

Plain woven cloth is often dyed in a dyebath. The cloth is passed backwards and forwards through the dye until the colour is strong enough.

loose yarn into thread. The thread is then dyed and knitted or spun into cloth. Knitted cotton makes stretchy clothes like T-shirts. Ordinary shirts are made from woven cotton.

At a clothing factory, workers have special jobs to get woven shirts ready. Spreaders lay out rolls, or bolts, of fabric on large tables. Markers outline a pattern on the cloth. Cutters snip out the pattern pieces. Sorters separate the pieces and sewers sew the shirts together. You might be wearing a T-shirt right now. How many people do you suppose worked on it before it got to you?

THINGS YOU WEAR

Zipping along

We can do up our clothes in all sorts of ways. Do you agree that a zip is one of the best? Zips were invented by Whitcomb L. Judson in America in 1893. He called his invention the slide fastener. It was used to do up shoes and it wasn't very reliable! The word zip was first used by a company in the 1920s. They made boots with side zips which they called 'zippers'.

The modern zip is made up of two lines of metal teeth fastened to a strip of fabric. The teeth on one side of the zip end in tiny balls. These slot into holes in the teeth on the other side. When you raise the slider of the zip, you push the teeth together. When you lower the slider, you force the teeth apart again.

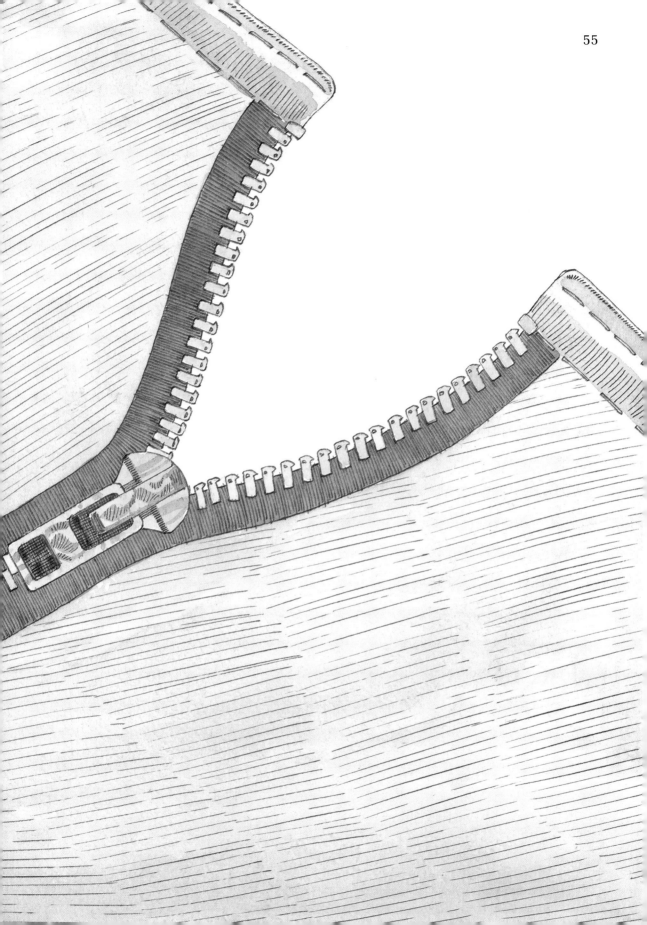

THINGS YOU WEAR

The first blue jeans

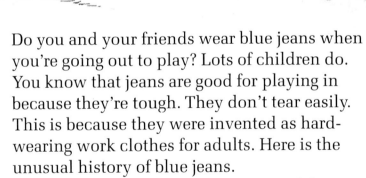

Do you and your friends wear blue jeans when you're going out to play? Lots of children do. You know that jeans are good for playing in because they're tough. They don't tear easily. This is because they were invented as hard-wearing work clothes for adults. Here is the unusual history of blue jeans.

The story of blue jeans started in California in the United States of America. In 1849, an important discovery of gold was made there. A lot of people rushed to California, hoping to become rich by finding gold. Miners sifted through rocky streams and muddy soil every day, looking for nuggets of gold.

Around 1853, an American businessman called Levi Strauss noticed how ragged and torn the miners' clothes were. He had an idea. He decided to make tough, new trousers which would stand up to the hard work of looking for gold. He made the trousers from canvas, a heavy cotton fabric which is used to make tents. The miners who tried the new trousers liked them because they were so strong. Strauss sold more and more. He even improved the trousers by using another fabric, a tough cotton called denim. Denim is dyed with a special blue dye called indigo, which gives it the blue jeans colour we all know.

In 1872, Strauss heard about a tailor named Jacob Davis. Davis was putting metal rivets along the pockets of miners' trousers. The rivets strengthened the trousers. Levi Strauss paid Jacob Davis to work for him, and soon they were making and selling riveted jeans. Today, jeans sell so well that you can buy them from lots of companies. But they are all based on Levi Strauss's first pair of jeans.

Jeans words

rivet
A rivet is a metal bolt which joins two metal plates together. The rivets which strengthen the seams in jeans' pockets are small and made of copper. But much larger rivets made of different metals can be used to join the metal sheets which make the bodies of ships and aeroplanes. These rivets make the metal strong and safe.

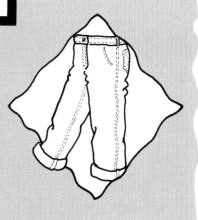

Surprising fibres

These clothes came from a pine tree and an oil well. Does that mean that someone found them in those places? Not exactly! It means that they were actually made from wood and oil. Did you know that chemical scientists can make fibres for cloth out of surprising things?

You already know that all cloth is made from fibres, the long, hair-like strands that can be spun into yarn. You know that some fibres grow naturally, such as those in sheep's wool or those found in a cotton boll. But there are other fibres — those made by people. We call these synthetic fibres.

How can you make a fibre? Let's look at a synthetic fibre called nylon. To make nylon, either oil or natural gas is treated with chemicals until the right blend of liquid forms. This liquid is then heated and forced into a machine that pumps it out through tiny holes. As soon as the thin streams of liquid hit the air, they harden into nylon fibres.

Rayon is another synthetic fibre. It is made from wood pulp, which is a mixture of wood chips and water that have been heated. The pulp is mixed with chemicals, heated and pressed through tiny openings in a machine. The rayon fibres form in the same way as nylon ones.

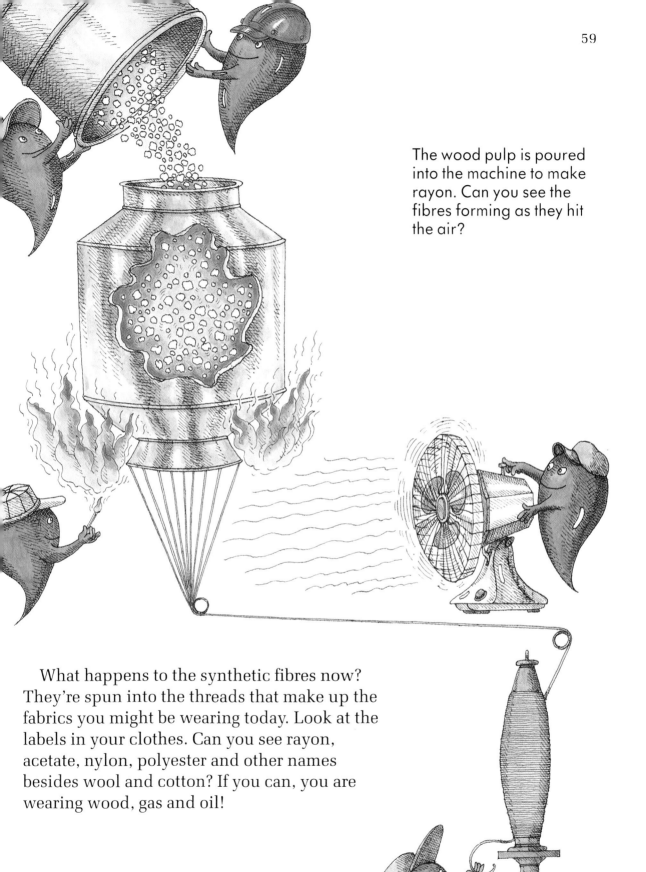

The wood pulp is poured into the machine to make rayon. Can you see the fibres forming as they hit the air?

What happens to the synthetic fibres now? They're spun into the threads that make up the fabrics you might be wearing today. Look at the labels in your clothes. Can you see rayon, acetate, nylon, polyester and other names besides wool and cotton? If you can, you are wearing wood, gas and oil!

THINGS YOU WEAR

The bouncing shoe

If you could have visited some Amazon Indians in Brazil as long ago as the 1700s, you might have thought there was something funny about their feet. They would have looked as though they were covered in rubber! That's because the Indians used to dip their feet in bowls of a milky substance which dripped from the cut bark of a certain tree. They let the substance dry on their feet. The 'shoes' that formed were a perfect fit and they were waterproof. When they had finished with the shoes, the Indians could just peel them off and throw them away.

These Amazon Indians made the first rubber shoes. The milky substance they used is called latex and it comes from the rubber tree. But when other people tried to copy the Indians and used latex straight from the tree like this, it melted in the heat and cracked in the cold. Then, in 1839, an American scientist called Charles Goodyear invented a process called vulcanization. This makes rubber strong and hard. Vulcanization means that the rubber we use to make sports shoes today is springy and tough.

In 1868, the first sports shoe with a rubber sole was made in the United States of America. It also had a canvas top and laces, and it became known as a 'sneaker' because it was so quiet to walk in. All sports shoes have developed from the pattern of this 'sneaker'.

Rubber words

vulcanization
Vulcanization is a way of mixing a chemical called sulphur with rubber. When rubber is heated with sulphur, the sulphur combines with the rubber to make it stronger. The more sulphur that is added, the stronger the rubber will be. The process of vulcanization can take a few minutes or several hours.

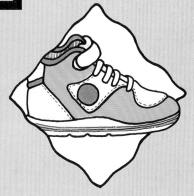

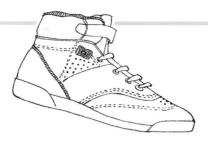

How sports shoes are made

First, the tops of the shoes, or uppers, are cut from canvas. Usually, a different person cuts each of the different parts. The cutters operate a machine that cuts the canvas just like a biscuit cutter cuts biscuits. The machine is called a die. Then other workers sew together all the parts for the upper.

canvas uppers

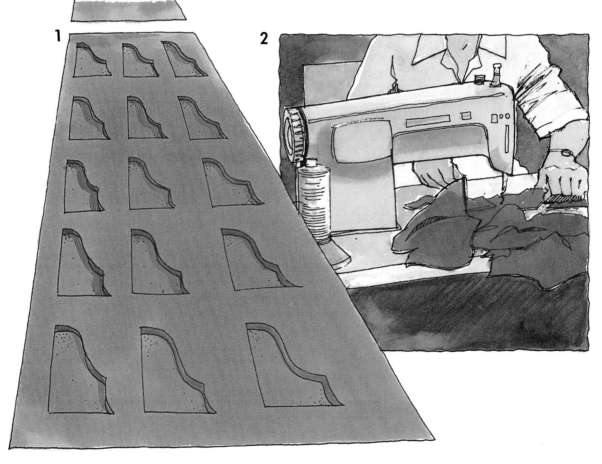

1

2

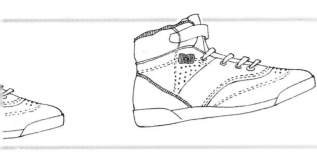 

Now the upper is shaped into a shoe on a metal or plastic mould called a last. The last gives the shoe the shape of a foot. The shoe is bathed in latex cement to make sure the parts stay together. A thin, rubber tape is wrapped around the bottom of the training shoe. The soles are prepared and attached, and the whole shoe goes into a machine that seals the soles to the upper.

last

3 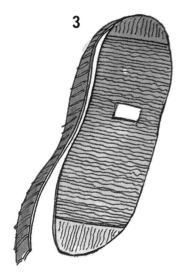 **4**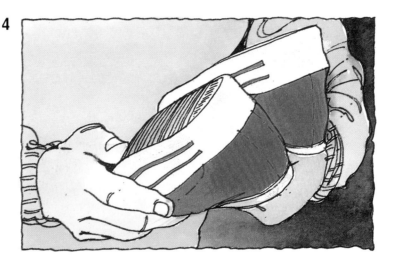

1. Cutting the uppers
2. Sewing the uppers
3. Attaching the rubber tape to the sole
4. Inspecting the shoes

Finally, the shoes are tested to make sure they are strong and flexible. An inspector makes sure that the two shoes match, left and right, and are the same size. The inspector may be the fiftieth person to work on that pair of sports shoes before they reach the shop!

things that keep you clean

How is soap made?
Who made the first toothbrush?
How clean is the air?

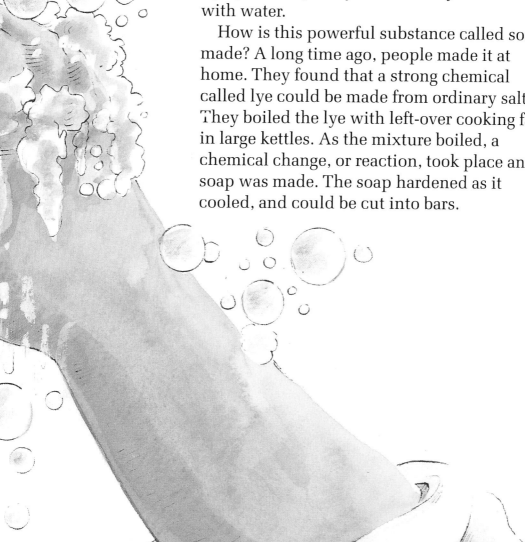

CLEANING UP

Dirt attack!

Watch out, dirt! That soap looks gentle but it's really an army of chemicals on the attack! When you wash your hands, the chemicals capture the dirt on them. They surround each piece of dirt and then break it up into smaller bits. And once these specks of dirt are broken up by the soap, they can be easily rinsed away with water.

How is this powerful substance called soap made? A long time ago, people made it at home. They found that a strong chemical called lye could be made from ordinary salt. They boiled the lye with left-over cooking fats in large kettles. As the mixture boiled, a chemical change, or reaction, took place and soap was made. The soap hardened as it cooled, and could be cut into bars.

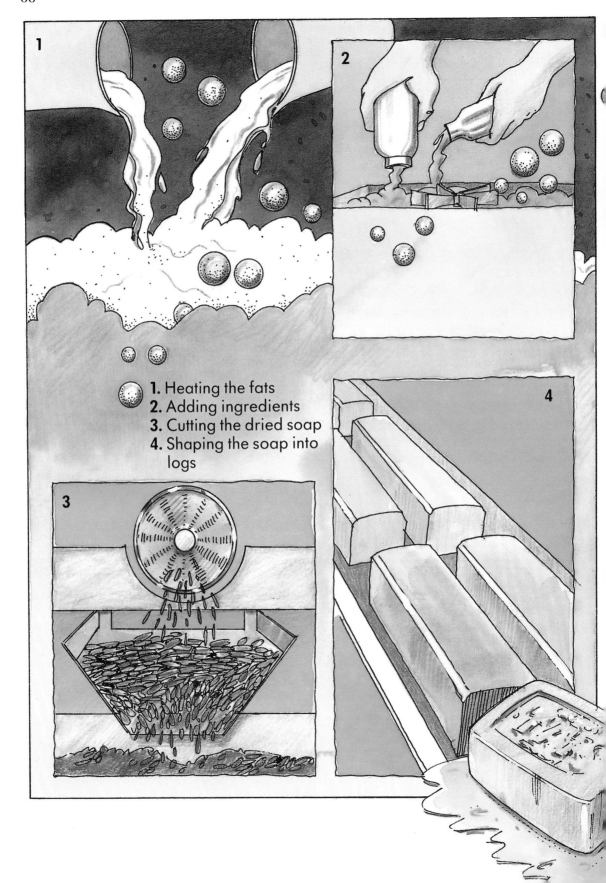

1. Heating the fats
2. Adding ingredients
3. Cutting the dried soap
4. Shaping the soap into logs

Soap words

acid
An acid is a type of chemical which can burn other materials. Strong acid can even burn through metal. Many acids are poisonous but some are found naturally in our bodies.

alkali
An alkali is a chemical which dissolves in water. Some alkalis are found in metals. Others are found as layers of chemical salts in dried up oceans.

Today we don't make our own soap. It is made by people, or manufactured, in different ways. One way to make soap is to heat animal fats or certain vegetable oils at very high temperatures. This causes the parts of the fat known as the fatty acids to separate from the rest of the mixture. Next, an ingredient is added to create a chemical reaction. That ingredient is caustic soda, another name for lye. The caustic soda mixes with the acids to form soap.

Now the soap is a thick, hot liquid. To this, colouring will be added, and possibly some perfume as well, before the mixture is dried in a machine called a vacuum chamber. The vacuum chamber sucks water out of the soap to completely dry it. Next is the noodle stage. This is where a cutting machine slices the dried soap into chunks that look like noodles.

Another machine shapes the noodles into long bars called logs. The logs look something like long loaves of bread. Bars of soap are cut from these logs and shaped.

Finally, the bars are wrapped. Each one is a neat package of chemicals ready to attack, surround, and capture dirt!

FUN TO DO
You can use manufactured soap to make paints which are just right for finger painting.

FUN TO DO

Soap paint

YOU WILL NEED:
1 cup soap powder
4 small bowls
4 tablespoons water
4 spoons
food colouring
thick drawing paper

* Ask your parents to
help you.

1. Pour about ¼ cup soap powder into each of the bowls.

2. Add a tablespoon of water to each bowl. Stir each mixture until thick.

3. Put 3-5 drops of food colouring into each bowl, using a different colour in each one.

**Remember not to put
soap in your mouth or
near your eyes.**

4. Blend the colours into
the flakes with a spoon.
Each mixture should be a
soft, soapy chunk.

5. Dip your fingers into
the mixture and dab it
onto your paper. You can
make a pattern or a
picture, changing colours
whenever you like.

Soap for your teeth

We don't use ordinary soap to clean our teeth, so what do we use instead? Toothpaste, of course. Hundreds of years ago, people did not have toothpaste. So they tried brushing their teeth with different ingredients, looking for a way to have clean, strong teeth. They even used crushed snail shells and powdered stones!

These ingredients sound strange to us today. But our toothpaste still contains some ingredients which come from shells and rocks! These ingredients come from natural substances called minerals. We call the minerals used in toothpaste polishing agents. They must be crushed finely so that they polish our teeth without scratching them.

Toothpaste words

mineral
Minerals are the thousands of different natural materials found in the earth. Minerals are made of substances that were never alive. Many of them, like rocks, are made of crystals. We use minerals to make many things — toothpaste is just one of them.

Other ingredients are added to toothpaste to keep it moist and to give it a pleasant taste. Small amounts of detergents give toothpaste its foam and a chemical called fluoride is added to help prevent tooth decay. But how do all these different ingredients get into the thin tube your toothpaste comes in? It happens at the factory.

First, the ingredients are mixed in a large machine until a paste is formed. The air is then removed and the paste is mixed once again so that it is completely smooth. Then the toothpaste is pumped into a funnel-shaped tank which is connected to the filler. The filler is a machine that fills the tubes.

Each tube is dropped with its cap pointing downwards into a holding cup on a turntable. The caps are on, but the bottoms of the tubes are open. The table turns and a nozzle moves down into the tube. The nozzle squirts out an exact amount of toothpaste.

Next, the turntable moves the tube so that it can be sealed. The ends of metal tubes are folded shut by a set of mechanical 'jaws'. If the tubes are plastic, the ends are melted shut by heated jaws.

Now it's time for the tubes to be pushed out of the holding cups and sent for packaging. Before long, the tubes are packed in boxes and sent to the shop, where customers can choose their favourite kind of toothpaste.

A horsehair toothbrush?

We need a toothbrush as well as toothpaste to clean our teeth properly. People used to clean their teeth with wooden sticks. Then, in the 1800s, an American doctor called Josiah Flagg invented a toothbrush. Flagg's brush had bristles made of horsehair, but other inventors used pig's bristles to make their toothbrushes. Today, millions of toothbrushes with nylon bristles are made each day. Here's how they are made.

The handles are made first. Coloured plastic crystals are melted and poured into moulds inside a machine. The hot plastic cools in seconds, forming the handles.

Then a worker feeds the finished handles into another machine. This machine grabs a bunch of nylon bristles and bends them in half to form a V shape. The machine then cuts off a tiny piece of metal and, in a flash, pushes the metal into the bend in the bristles. Lastly, the metal and bristles are pushed into each hole of the handle. When the bristles are cut and smoothed, the toothbrush is finished.

Cleaning up an ocean

Water from rain and rivers has to be cleaned so that it is safe for you to wash in and to drink. You don't drink the salty water from oceans, but sometimes that needs cleaning too.

Large ships travel across the oceans, carrying cargo from one country to another. If a ship carrying an oil like petroleum has an accident, large amounts of oil can be spilled into the water. Oil won't mix with water, so it floats on the surface in huge sheets called oil slicks. An oil spill is one of the worst kinds things that can happen to an ocean. Oil slicks kill sea birds and animals and spoil beaches. When people makes their surroundings dirty like this, we call it pollution.

Oil has been washed up from the sea to pollute this beach.

Oil words

petroleum
Petroleum is oil that is found in layers under the earth and oceans. These layers are called reserves. Scientists think that petroleum formed from the remains of tiny animals that died millions of years ago. The process that produced petroleum also produced natural gas. Petroleum is one of the most valuable natural minerals in the world. It provides fuel for our homes and power for our cars and trucks.

Oil pollution is hard to get rid of. One of the best ways of cleaning up an ocean polluted with oil comes from nature. Tiny living things called micro-organisms can help do the job. A micro-organism is so small that you can only see one through a high-powered microscope. Micro-organisms 'eat' oil. They break it down into small particles so that it can be washed away.

Micro-organisms eat oil fastest when it is spread thinly across the water's surface. Sometimes waves whip oil slicks into a foam which is nicknamed 'mousse'. The mousse is made of large globs of oil which the micro-organisms find hard to break down. The micro-organisms also find it hard to work if the weather is cold. Oil does not spread out in cold water as quickly as it does in warmer water.

Booms made of floating foam tubes help to keep the oil in one place.

This skimming machine has a moving belt that the oil sticks to.

So what happens to the big globs of oil or the oil which is spilled in cold water? People have to try to clean it up themselves. Clean-up workers try to keep the oil in one place. They put floating barriers, or booms, into the water. These can help stop the oil from spreading if the water is calm.

Sometimes clean-up workers skim oil away instead of soaking it up. Think of a cook skimming fat off the top of a soup with a spoon. Skimming machines do a similar job with oil. Some skimmers have special parts attached which the oil sticks to. Others spin the water and oil around until the oil separates from the water. Then workers pump the skimmed oil into tanks.

Sometimes oil is burned off the surface of the ocean, but this burning can cause air pollution.

Chemicals sprayed onto the oil break it up into thinner patches.

Sometimes clean-up workers even set the oil on fire to burn it away. They use torches or lasers to start the fire. Lasers are machines that shoot out beams of light. The beams create heat. Sometimes they add chemicals that break up the oil. Then waves spread the oil around so that micro-organisms can eat it.

You can see that there are lots of ways to clean up an ocean polluted with oil. But an oil spill is almost impossible to clean up completely. No matter how hard people work, some oil is left in the ocean and on the beaches. But scientists are working to try to make the best ocean cleaning method, nature's micro-organisms, even more effective for the future.

FUN TO DO
You know that oil floats on the surface of water. You can use floating oil to make your own coloured paper.

FUN TO DO

Marbled paper

YOU WILL NEED:
oil-based paint of different
   colours
several sheets of white
   paper
a large baking tin
paint thinner, such as white
   spirit or turpentine
water
glass jars
newspaper
an apron
a pencil

**This can get messy, so
cover your clothes with
an apron and your work
surface with newspaper.**

1. Choose two or more colours of paint and put each one in a jar. Add the thinner until the paint is watery. To begin with, try mixing one part thinner with one part paint.

2. Fill the baking tin with water about two centimetres deep. Drop in a little paint and let it float to the surface of the water. Then swirl it around with the end of your pencil. Carefully swirl in another colour, until you have a pattern you like.

Remember!
Paint thinners are poisonous,
so ask an adult to help you.

4. Try adding different colours. You can use thicker paint with thin paint, or make blank spaces with drops of thinner. Change the water when the colours become mixed together and it looks 'muddy'. You can use your rainbow paper as writing paper or wrapping paper.

Don't pour your muddy mixture down the drain! Instead, pour it into an empty container and put it in the dustbin.

3. Gently place a piece of paper flat on the surface of the water and paint mixture. The oily paint swirls will stick to the paper at once, so take the paper out again straight away. Peel it away carefully from the liquid. Let it drip for a few seconds and then lay it out to dry.

CLEANING UP

How clean is our air?

Here you are, walking along a busy street in town. A long line of cars moves slowly along the road, stopping and starting as the traffic lights change, their engines chugging and roaring. You can see how dirty the air is, and sometimes the fumes can make you cough and sneeze. At last you reach the park. The air smells fresher and cleaner away from the traffic.

Cars and trucks in every street cause air pollution by puffing out harmful substances into the air. Tiny particles of the metal lead are released when cars burn petrol with lead in it. Lead is harmful to living things.

You may not have heard of nitrogen oxide, but you may have learned about acid rain. Acid rain is one of the bad effects of air pollution. Fumes from car exhausts, power stations and factories contain a dangerous chemical called nitrogen oxide. When the fumes rise into the air, they mix with water vapour to form nitric acid. The nitric acid falls back to earth when it rains and is washed down into the soil as acid rain. Trees and other plants cannot live in soil which has become too acid. In some parts of the world, whole forests are dying. And when acid rain falls into lakes, most of the animals and plants that live in and around the lakes die.

The greenhouse effect

The fuels we use to give us energy for heat and light can also cause air pollution. When any substance which contains the chemical called carbon is burned, it gives off a gas called carbon dioxide. Oil and coal contain carbon so they release carbon dioxide into the air when they are burned in power stations.

What happens to all this carbon dioxide? It rises into the Earth's atmosphere and forms a kind of shield, trapping the Sun's heat near the Earth. We call this the 'greenhouse effect' because the shield is acting like the glass in a greenhouse. Just like the inside of a greenhouse, the Earth is gradually becoming warmer and warmer.

"Great!" you might say, "There'll be long, hot summers every year!" But sadly, it won't be as simple as that. If the Earth carries on warming up, this is what will happen. As the years pass, the ice at the North Pole and South Pole will slowly begin to melt and the sea-level will rise. Low-lying parts of the Earth will be flooded. Cities and towns may disappear and people will have to move elsewhere. Hot, dry parts of the Earth will become hotter and drier. More and more land will become desert. Many kinds of animal and plant will die out and people may not have enough to eat.

Lead, acid rain, the greenhouse effect... It all seems like bad news. The good news is that we can all do something today to stop these things polluting our planet.

Can we stop air pollution?

Huge steps have already been taken to stop lead pollution. Unleaded petrol is now available in many countries and people use it in their cars if they can. Some cars won't run on unleaded petrol, so governments all over the world need to make laws to change the way cars are made.

Scientists have found ways of cleaning the smoke that pours into the air from car exhausts and factory chimneys. Something called a catalytic converter can be fitted to cars to filter out the chemicals that cause acid rain. Coal can be cleaned even before it's burned in factories and power stations. Or the smoke can be filtered before it reaches the open air.

And what about the greenhouse effect? We can stop burning carbon when it's not really necessary. Cars don't have to run on petrol or diesel. Clean fuels, such as methane or alcohol, can be just as good. And power stations and factories can run on other kinds of energy, such as solar power from the Sun, or power from water.

You can do something to help, too. Walk or go by bicycle instead of by car whenever you can. Turn lights off when you don't need them. Think about ways of saving energy all the time. Help to keep our air clean!

Carbon dioxide from factories traps the Sun's rays. The heat can't escape and the Earth warms up.

FIND OUT ABOUT

things that help you to learn

Where does paper come from?
How does the lead get inside a pencil?
What makes a computer work?

How ideas become books

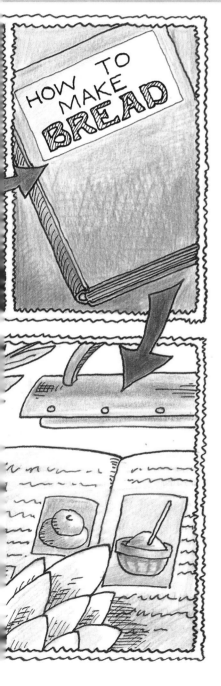

It feels good to open a book. As you flip through the pages, the words and pictures invite you to join in a wonderful new adventure. Or, in books like this one, the pages help you to find out about all kinds of subjects. Have you ever wondered about how books are made? They start with ideas.

The writer, or author, has a good idea for a story or a factual book. Little Red Hen has an idea for a book about making bread. She writes to a publishing company about her idea, and sends a typed copy of the book she has written. This typed copy is called a manuscript.

An editor at the publishing company decides if the book will be interesting for other people to read. The editor at this company likes Little Red Hen's manuscript. Her book is going to be published! Little Red Hen goes to the office to talk to the editor. The editor suggests some changes she would like made to the book, and Little Red Hen agrees.

When the manuscript is finished, the editor checks it and then it is marked with special codes. The codes show how the words should look when they're printed.

The manuscript is sent to another company, called a typesetting company. Here, the coded manuscript is typed into a computer. The computer produces long pages of words or text, called galleys. These are sent back to the publisher where a proofreader reads one set of the galleys and uses special marks to show any mistakes. Final pages of text are then made by the typesetter. The pages are produced as film, just like the film your photos are on before they are developed.

Meanwhile, a designer at the publishing company decides how the book will look by making a plan, or layout, of each page. Little Red Hen goes into the office again to talk about the pictures for the book with the designer and the editor. They talk about what the pictures will look like with the artist. The artist sends pencil drawings of the pictures first, to be sure they're right. Once the editor and designer have checked the pencil sketches, the artist draws his final pictures and sends them in.

Then a machine called a scanner photographs the artist's pictures. The machine makes the pictures into film, too. This is put together with the text film onto thin sheets of metal called printing plates. The plates are pressed against the film and exposed to light. The text and the picture images that were on the film move onto the plates. The plates are used to print the book.

Book words

editor
An editor is the person who must make sure that the author's manuscript is correct and ready to be published. The editor checks spelling, grammar and punctuation. Sometimes editors add to the manuscript, or take parts out of it. Editors must also check that all the author's facts are correct.

designer
A designer has to decide on the overall look of the book. The designer looks at the text and the artist's pictures and puts them together in the most attractive way. The designer also decides how the cover of the book will look.

At last Little Red Hen's book can be printed! The plates are slotted into a machine called a printing press and coated with ink. They transfer the ink to large rollers inside the press. These rollers then print the images onto book paper which is fed through the press.

The press cuts all the printed sheets of the book into smaller sheets and folds them into a section of pages. Then it gathers the sections into the right order. The sections are glued or sewn together by another machine.

Lastly, the book needs a cover. The cover is printed separately from the book pages and glued onto sturdy cardboard. Another machine then presses and pastes the end sheets of the book to the cover.

Little Red Hen's book is finished! Thousands of copies just like the first one will be printed so that all Little Red Hen's friends will be able to find out how bread is made.

Cooking wood for paper

Tear a small piece of tissue or newspaper. Look at it closely. Can you see tiny fibres on the torn edge? If you look at the torn edge under a microscope, you'll see that the paper fibres look like a bundle of straw that has been pressed flat.

The fibre in paper is called cellulose. It is found in all types of plants. Paper gets its name from a reed called papyrus that the Ancient Egyptians used to make a kind of paper. Today the cellulose in paper comes from trees. Here's what happens.

To make paper, tree farmers called foresters first choose trees for cutting. Forests are looked after carefully and two or three new trees are planted for every tree that is cut down for papermaking. Huge saws remove the branches. The logs are sent to a paper mill.

Here the logs are fed into a large machine that scrapes off their bark. A moving belt then carries the logs to another machine that cuts them into small pieces about two centimetres long. The pieces are called wood chips.

Next, the wood chips are boiled with water and chemicals in a huge tank. The boiled chips turn into a soft mush called pulp. The pulp is then washed and bleached clean. In a machine called a refiner, the pulp is beaten so that the fibres break up and fray at the edges. Then the refined pulp flows down a pipe to a big rolling belt made of wire mesh. The screen moves along a track and shakes from side to side. This locks the fibres together. The water drains away through holes at the bottom. The pulp left on top of the screen is wet paper.

chipping

cleaning

refining

draining

drying

rolling

Now comes the ironing process. The wet paper flows between huge rollers that squeeze out more water. Then the paper passes over and under heated rollers to dry it. Still more rollers press and smooth the paper surface.

When the paper is dry, it is wound into huge rolls. A pile of these rolls can reach as high as the second floor of a building! The rolls will be cut into sheets which can be used to make newspapers, stamps, books ... Can you think of any more things made from paper?

Will we always have enough trees to make paper for all these things? We hope so! Using paper more than once is one way to avoid wasting trees. We call this recycling paper. See if there is a recycling centre in the place where you live. At a recycling centre, old paper is collected and sent back to the mills. Then it can be boiled down and made into new paper. So if you take your old newspapers to a recycling centre, you can save a tree!

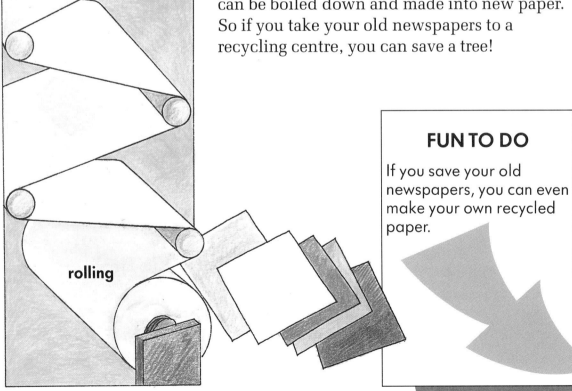

FUN TO DO

If you save your old newspapers, you can even make your own recycled paper.

FUN TO DO

Recycled paper

YOU WILL NEED:

3 tissues
hot water
a bowl
a hand whisk
a square baking tin
a rolling pin
newspaper
¼ cup of liquid starch
wire mesh, edges folded,
to fit in baking tin
a teatowel

* Ask your parents to
help you.

1. Tear the tissues into small pieces, about the size of postage stamps. Drop them into the bowl and add a cup of hot water.

2. Beat the mixture until it's smooth. There should be no big pieces left.

3. Stir in the liquid starch. Then pour the mixture into the baking tin.

4. Dip the mesh into the tin, sliding it under the mixture. Move the mesh around to get a thin, even layer of mixture on top. Use your fingers to spread the mixture out evenly.

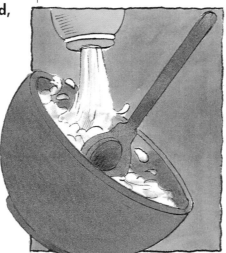

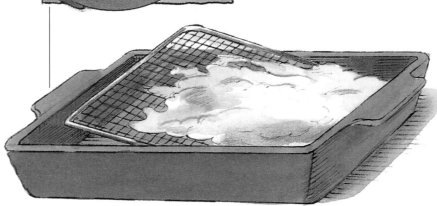

Remember!
Don't drink liquid starch.
It is poisonous.

7. Roll a rolling pin over the newspaper to blot your paper.

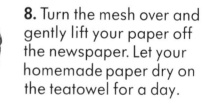

5. Lift the mesh straight up out of the tin and let the water drain away.

6. Lay the mesh between the pages of a newspaper.

8. Turn the mesh over and gently lift your paper off the newspaper. Let your homemade paper dry on the teatowel for a day.

A wooden sandwich

Did you know that the pencil you use every day is made in the same way that you would make a sandwich? The lead is the filling of the sandwich. Two slats of wood go round the outside, just like the two slices of bread in a real sandwich!

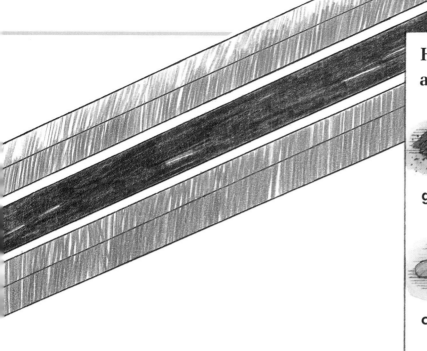

How pencil leads are made

graphite

clay

water

heat

wax

The lead in your pencil is not really made of lead. Long ago, people did use sticks of lead to write with, but now we use graphite. Graphite is a soft mineral that comes from mines underground.

To make the pencil lead, graphite is mixed with clay and water in a huge tank. Then the mixture is put into a machine that makes it into sticks that look like licorice. The sticks are cut into pieces and baked in a hot oven. Then they're cooled and dipped in wax. The wax helps the pencil write smoothly on paper.

So that's the inside of the wooden sandwich. The outside is usually made from cedar wood. Cedar is an ideal wood for pencils because it is soft. That makes it easy to sharpen.

This picture shows all the stages of making a pencil.

First, cedar logs are sawn into thin slats. Then the slats are stained, waxed and dried. Next, machines cut narrow grooves in each slat. After glue is spread over one slat, a stick of graphite is placed in each groove, and another slat is pressed tightly over it.

A clamp holds each slat 'sandwich' together until the glue dries. Then the pressed slats go through a cutting machine that cuts them into single pencils. Finally, the pencils are ready for painting. If erasers are needed, they go on after painting, capping each pencil in a thin, metal holder.

And that is how a pencil is made. The next time you write a letter, or do your homework, think of your trusty wooden sandwich and how it helps you with your writing every day!

How chalk is made

Do you remember the first time you wrote on a blackboard? It was fun making large, white letters with a chunky piece of chalk. If you made a mistake, it was no trouble to rub it out and try again.

You already know a few things about chalk. It's white or pastel-coloured. It breaks easily. And it's dusty. That's because chalk is made from soft minerals.

The main ingredients in chalk are calcium carbonate, clay and water. For pastel chalk, coloured powders are added. In the chalk factory, those ingredients are mixed together in a huge mixing machine.

The chalk mixture is a soft paste which is squeezed out of the machine through a narrow opening. It comes out looking like sausage-shaped tubes. Sometimes it is poured into moulds that shape it into the chalk sticks we use.

Chalk words

Plaster of Paris
Plaster of Paris is a fine, white powder made by heating a mineral called gypsum. But why is this gypsum powder named after a famous city? The answer is it's because many gypsum mines are found near Paris in France.

Next the tubes are baked. You can bake chalk in much the same way as you bake biscuits. The tubes are cut into sticks, or the chalk is emptied from the moulds. The cut or moulded pieces are slid into an oven on trays. Then the chalk is baked for about six hours.

When the sticks are cool, they are counted by machine and put into boxes. By the time it gets to you, the chalk is ready for anything from drawing on the blackboard to marking the pavement for a game.

FUN TO DO

You can use plaster of Paris to make your own chalk.

FUN TO DO

Home-made chalk

YOU WILL NEED:

2 tablespoons of plaster of
 Paris (from a craft or
 hardware shop)
2 tablespoons of water
a small plastic sandwich
 bag
a paper cup
a mixing spoon
2 clothes-pegs
clothes-line or hanger
food colouring (optional)

* Ask your parents to
help you.

1. Mix the water and plaster of Paris in the paper cup.

2. Mix in a few drops of food colouring if you like.

3. Pour the mixture into the bag.

4. Roll down the top edge of the bag, moulding the mixture into a tube shape.

5. Clip the closed bag to a clothes-line or hanger. Keep the tube straight.

6. Wait for a day for the plaster to harden. Unwrap your chalk and let it dry another day or so before using it.

Remember!
Don't put plaster of Paris
in your mouth.
It is poisonous.

Thinking machines

Have you ever used a computer to help with your schoolwork? If you have, you will already know a lot of the things that computers can do. They can ask you questions. They can tell you if your answers are right or wrong. They can work out problems for you, and they can even say goodbye when you've finished. It's almost as if these marvellous machines could think for themselves!

If a computer could think, it would need to have a brain. Of course, machines don't have a brain like we have. But the computer does have a special piece of machinery which controls it, just as your brain controls you. The computer's 'brain' is a microchip called the main chip. A microchip is a tiny device that is smaller than your fingernail!

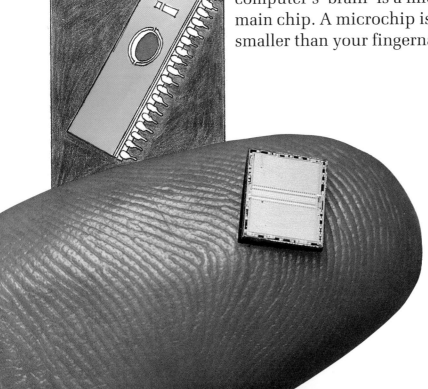

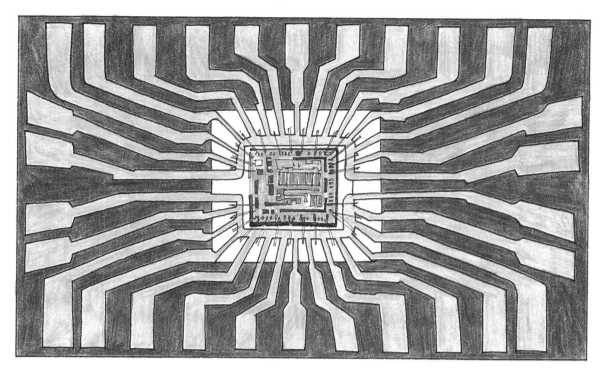

A microchip is made from a material called silicon. Its surface is cut with tiny grooves, all of which are packed with many thousands of tiny electrical switches. The switches are connected by thin metal wires called electrical pathways. All the pathways link together to make a group called a circuit. When you use the computer, bursts of electricity move along the circuits at great speed. These bursts are like messages. They tell the computer what to do.

The messages are sent to the main chip by a package of step-by-step instructions called a program. The main chip then acts like a police officer directing traffic. It controls the flow of electric signals from one part of the computer to another. Other chips, called memory chips, help the main chip. The memory chips hold information for the computer to process.

There are hundreds of electrical pathways making up a circuit on the surface of each microchip.

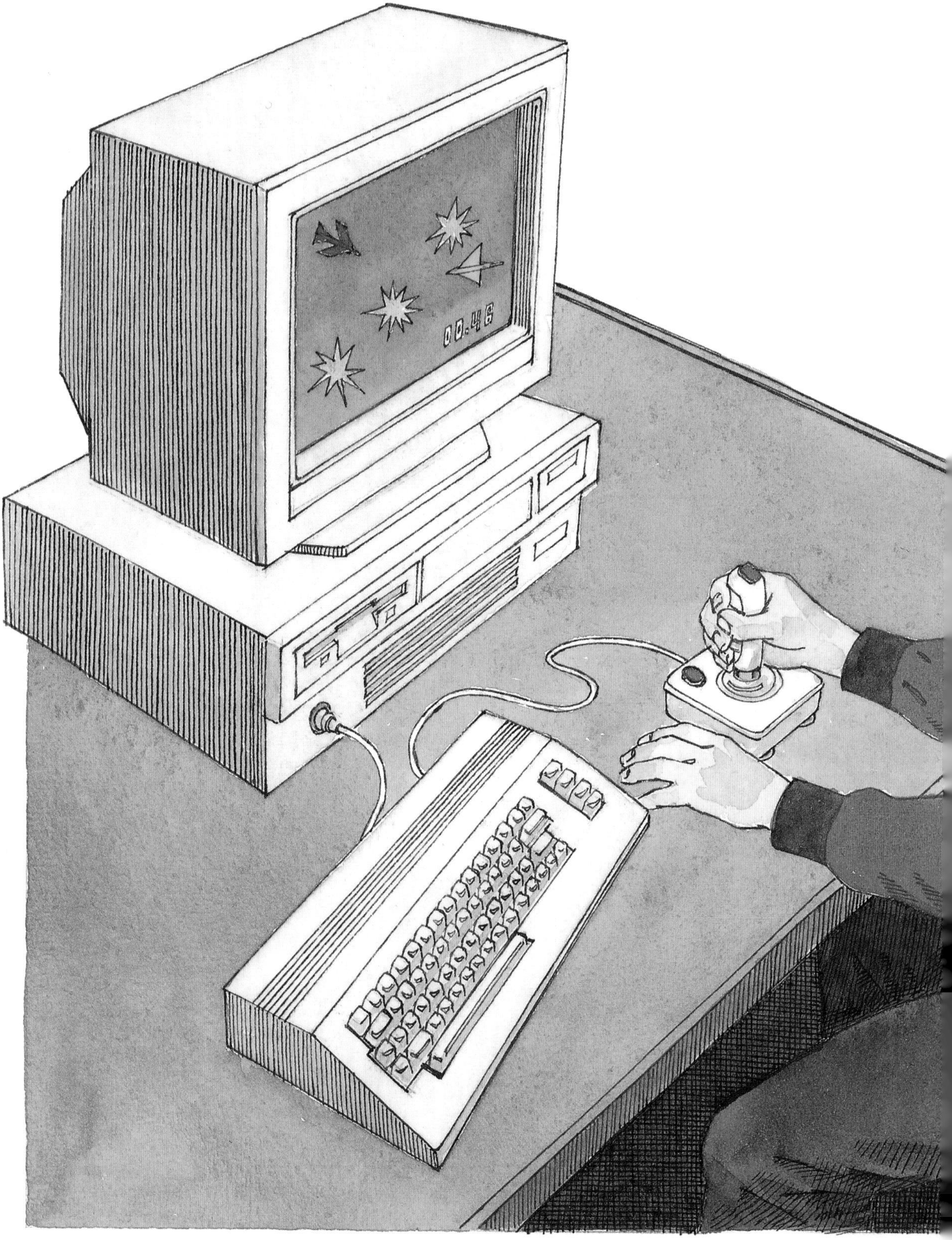
00.46

How does the computer get the information? It has to be told. You can tell the computer what to do by typing in letters and numbers on a keyboard. Or the computer can read information from a disk you slot into it.

The computer shows you the results of its work on a screen. The screen is called the visual display unit, or VDU for short. If you've played computer games, you know how quickly the computer can send information to the screen. The pictures you see are changing all the time! This is because computers work at lightning speed. The main chip can do millions of jobs in one second. So even though a computer doesn't have a real brain, it can think quickly and accurately to help you work out problems, and have fun at the same time!

Passing the time

What's the time? You probably ask that question at least once a day. And it's easy for you to find out the answer. But if you'd lived thousands of years ago, you'd have found it much more difficult to find out the time.

People who lived in prehistoric times, used the sun to tell them the time of day. Prehistoric people watched the shadows made by the sun as it moved across the sky. When the shadows were short, they knew that the sun was directly overhead so it was the middle of the day. When the shadows were long, the day was either beginning or ending.

Clock words

pendulum
A pendulum swings backwards and forwards naturally because of gravity. Gravity is a force which pulls objects towards the earth. Gravity makes a pendulum swing at the same speed all the time, which is why it can be used to measure time inside a clock.

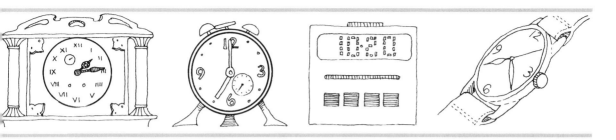

This is a picture of an Ancient Egyptian water clock.

If you had been an Ancient Egyptian, you would have used a water clock to tell you the time. The Egyptians used a stone bucket with a set of numbers, called a scale, marked on the inside. Water trickled out of the bucket through a hole in the bottom at a steady rate. As the water drained away, the scale measured the water level to show how much time had passed.

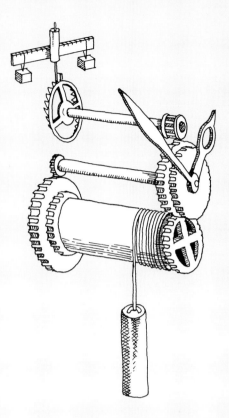

As the weight falls, it sets the wheel moving round. This makes the clock hands move round, too.

FUN TO DO

Find out how to make a water clock just like an Ancient Egyptian one.

What first put the tick-tock sound in clocks? It was a mechanical movement invented in Europe nearly 700 years ago. A wheel and a balance were connected to the clock hands and a weight was attached to the wheel. As the weight fell, it moved the wheel round in a series of jerks, or ticks. The turning of the wheel moved the hands round.

In the 1600s another type of clock was invented. This clock used a round weight which swung backwards and forwards. We call this kind of weight a pendulum and the new clocks were called pendulum clocks.

Inside a pendulum clock there is a curved metal bar at the top called an anchor escapement. It rocks backwards and forwards to keep the swing of the pendulum under control. A falling weight at the bottom of the clock sets the pendulum swinging. As the pendulum swings, the anchor rocks. One after the other, the ends of the anchor catch in a toothed wheel. The toothed wheel turns another, much smaller wheel. This is the escape wheel and it makes the clock hands tick round ... Tick, tock; tick, tock.

Today, many clocks are electrical. But you may still have a mechanical clock or a pendulum clock in your home. You may also have a clock that you carry with you wherever you go. It's called a watch, of course!

A water clock

YOU WILL NEED:

two plastic cups
a small nail
a long ruler
a marker pen
strong adhesive tape
modelling clay
a watch or clock with a
    second hand

* Ask your parents to
help you.

1. With the nail, pierce a small hole in the middle of the bottom of one of the plastic cups.

2. Make a scale on the inside of the other cup by drawing lines half a centimetre apart.

3. Using plenty of adhesive tape, stick the two cups to the ruler, one above the other. The cup marked with the scale should be at the bottom. Stick a large lump of modelling clay to your working surface. Use this to keep the ruler standing firmly upright.

4. Put a finger over the hole in the bottom of the cup. Fill the cup with water. Take your finger away and let the water drip out. Note how long it takes for the water to reach each of the marks on the bottom cup. Now try and make a water clock with a scale of marks one minute apart.

FIND OUT ABOUT

things
you play with

What makes some toys move and talk?
When were roller skates invented?
How are crayons made?

Toys that move and talk

Do you have any toys that talk or move by themselves? You may have seen a doll that can open its eyes, turn its head to look at you, and even speak! Or you may have a model computer that can ask you questions and tell you the right answer.

Amazing toys like these are powered by electricity. They are called electronic toys. The doll can talk and move because it is powered by electricity. The electrical power is made by a battery inside its body. The battery sends electricity to a small tape cassette inside the body and the voice plays. It moves because there are wires inside its body which are controlled by electricity sent from the battery.

Toys like the model computer are controlled by batteries and a tiny electronic device called a microchip. We use microchips to help make toys which can do more than ever before.

This electronic toy uses a speech synthesizer powered by a microchip to talk to you.

When you turn the model computer on, electricity races out of the battery along a wire to the chip. The electricity moves through the chip, making switches open and close. The switches control what the toy can do.

Remember the computer that can ask questions? It can talk because it has a special machine inside it called a speech synthesizer. To synthesize means to put together. Sounds are put together to sound like a real voice. So if the toy says the word 'book', for example, one signal from the microchip has first instructed the synthesizer to make a 'b' sound. The next signal from the chip has told it to make an 'oo' sound. Then the toy is told to make a 'k' sound. The sounds run together to make the word 'book'.

So next time you're playing with an electronic toy, remember the battery or microchip that brings it to life for you.

Electronic toy words

battery
A battery is a small container made of the metal zinc. In the middle is a rod made of a chemical called carbon. Between the rod and the zinc case is a paste made of other chemicals.

When the toy is turned on, an electric current flows out of the battery, into the toy and back into the battery.

Biking it

You might think a bike is a simple machine. You hop on, turn the pedals, and off you zoom! But bikes are cleverly designed. Inventors have worked hard to produce the bikes we know today.

It wasn't always easy to hop on a bike and pedal away. In the 1870s an Englishman named J. Starley invented a bicycle called the Penny Farthing. This early bike had a large front wheel — up to 1.5 metres high — and a very small back wheel. It was hard to climb onto the bicycle and even harder to balance while riding along! The rider could be thrown off if the bike hit a bump in the road.

Today's bikes are much more comfortable and safe to ride than the Penny Farthing. Each part has an important purpose. Look at a bike's frame. The steel tubes are strong enough to let you ride on any bumpy surface.

There's not much danger of falling off your bike, as long as you ride safely.

What about the other parts? Special notched wheels called gears mean that you can ride a bike faster than you can run. The notches fit into other notches on the bike chain. When you push your foot down on the pedal, the pedal turns the large front gear. This gear pushes the chain round.

The chain moves a smaller gear on the back wheel. For every one push you make on the pedal, the two gears move the back wheel around two, three or even four times. If you have a bike with several gears, you can change speeds by switching gear.

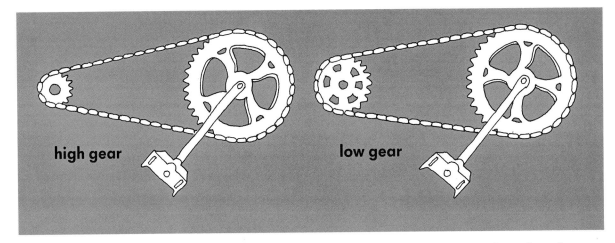

high gear **low gear**

At high gear speeds, used for riding level or downhill, the back gear is small. One turn of the large front gear can turn it round many times. This means that you can pedal slowly. At lower gear speeds, the back gear is larger. One turn of the front gear turns the back gear only a few times so that it is easier to pedal if you are going uphill or against the wind.

Riding a bicycle is good exercise because you are the engine. Your feet make the power to push the wheels round. Safe riding!

THINGS YOU PLAY WITH

The tale of the kite

There is a legend which tells of a Chinese general who wanted to attack a walled city. The general made a battle plan. He ordered his soldiers to dig a tunnel up to the wall and underneath it. Then his army would be able to crawl through the tunnel and into the city.

But how long did the tunnel need to be? The entrance to the city was some distance away and the general did not dare approach closer to find out. So the clever general sent up a kite and marked the string when the kite hovered over the city. The length of the string told him how far to dig the tunnel. The plan worked, and the general captured the city.

Kites have had other starring roles in history. In 1752, the American scientist Benjamin Franklin flew a kite with a metal key attached to the string during a thunderstorm. Franklin wanted to prove that lightning is an electric force. When lightning struck the key, it caused a spark and Franklin knew he was right. Other people have experimented with kites to test weather conditions and to try out ideas for making aeroplanes.

Most of the kites we see today are made to be flown for fun. They can be beautiful or unusual shapes, from a simple diamond-shape to the complicated box shaped-kite. But all kites are made in the same way. They have a frame made of rods, or struts, covered with fabric.

The long string, or line, that you hold is attached to the kite by two or more lines called the bridle. The bridle makes sure the kite is always pointing upwards and into the wind. The tail is attached to the end of the kite and helps to keep it pointed towards the sky.

To fly a kite, find an open space like a field or a park. Stand with your back to the wind and ask a friend to throw the kite up into the air. Keep the line straight as the kite soars up into the sky. When you get used to your kite, you can try using the line to make your kite perform acrobatics. Then you can watch it soar and dive like a bird!

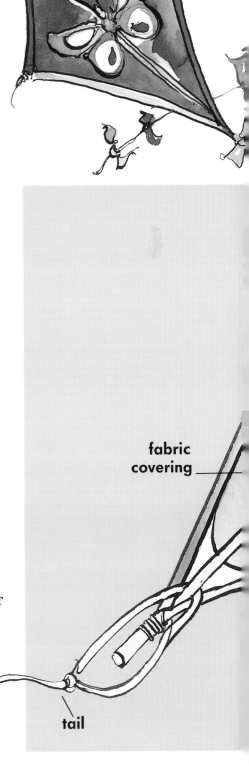

fabric covering

tail

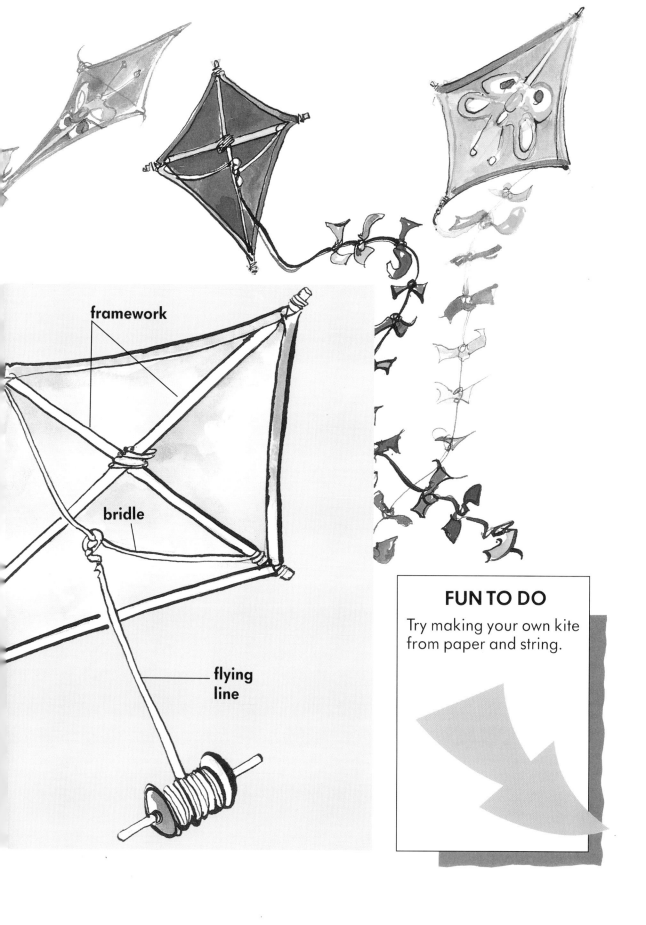

framework

bridle

flying
line

FUN TO DO

Try making your own kite
from paper and string.

A paper kite

YOU WILL NEED:
1 sheet of thick paper
scissors
a hole punch
paper reinforcement
   rings
a ball of string
1 tissue
1 small paper clip
a ruler

* **Ask your parents to help you.**

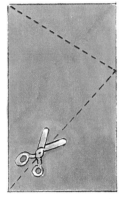

1. Fold the paper in half. Make a diamond shape by cutting a small triangle off the upper corner of the open edge and a larger triangle off the lower corner of the same edge.

2. Punch holes inside the left, right and bottom corners of the diamond. Stick reinforcement rings over the holes.

3. To make the bridle, cut a piece of string about 45 centimetres long. Thread the ends of the string through the holes in the left and right corners of the diamond. Tie large knots in each end to stop the bridle from slipping out.

4. For the tail, cut another piece of string about 50 centimetres long. Then cut the tissue into four strips. Make bows by gently tying the sections onto the tail string. Leave about 8 centimetres between each bow. Tie the tail to the bottom of the kite.

5. Attach a paper clip to the bridle. Tie the spool of string to the paper clip. Now you can fly your kite.

THINGS
YOU PLAY
WITH

A good skate

Ready, steady, go!
Roller skating is
a fun way to move
around.

Race, then glide. Race, then glide. It only takes a few hours and a couple of falls to get used to new roller skates. Then you can skate with your friends — it's much faster than walking!

Skating wasn't always this easy. The first roller skates were invented by ice skaters who had to give up their favourite sport each time the weather got warmer and the ice melted. So they tried to replace the blades on their skates with wheels. One of the first kinds of skate had two wheels under each shoe. But there was no way to turn or stop and it was very easy to fall over!

Roller skating became more popular in the late 1800s. New skates had been invented which had a pair of wooden wheels attached to the front and back of each skate. The wheels were mounted on blocks so that skaters could turn easily.

But the new skates still weren't perfect. The straps used to attach the skates to shoes were uncomfortable and they broke easily. Metal clamps had to be added to keep the skates on. Skaters tightened and loosened the clamps with skate keys.

Skates kept changing through the years. At one time metal soles were made to fit below the shoes. The size of the soles could be changed according to the size of the skater's feet. Metal wheels replaced wooden ones.

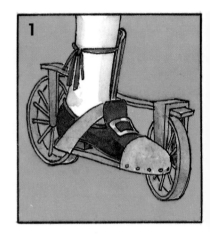

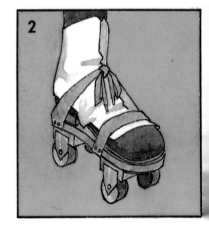

1. Wooden skates from 1780
2. Wooden skates from 1863
3. Metal skates from 1940
4. Metal skates from 1970

Roller skate words

ball bearings

Ball bearings are small metal balls which keep the moving parts of the wheel turning smoothly. The wheels are attached to a metal bar called an axle. As the axle turns the wheels, it rubs against the ball bearings instead of scraping directly against the wheel. The ball bearings can roll round and round inside the wheel.

Today, if you have roller skates, the wheels are probably made of strong plastic. The wheels have small metal balls called ball bearings inside them to keep you gliding along smoothly and quietly.

You will probably also find a piece of plastic called a toe stop across the front of your skate. You can use the toe stop to stop suddenly without falling over. Your skates probably have comfortable straps or even a leather boot instead of clamps. Thanks to all these improvements over the years, you can just keep rolling along!

Splashing colours

Do you know what all the objects in the pictures on this page have in common? They have all been used to make paint. Paint has been used since people first lived on Earth. Early people used soot to make black paint. They probably made yellow paint from flowers and browns and reds from powdered clay.

We call colours made from natural objects like these, pigments. The first paint makers ground pigments between stones to make powders. Then they mixed the powders with melted beeswax, animal fat, or animal blood. These bound the powders into a paste which spread easily and stuck onto a surface well. Stone Age people used these colours to paint pictures on the walls of their caves.

These people probably experimented with lots of materials to make different colours. They found out how to mix pigments to make new colours. They mixed red and blue to make purple and yellow and blue to make green.

Later, artists mixed their pigments with water or eggs. Then, in the 1400s, European painters began using oil as a binder to mix ingredients together. They also added sticky liquids called resins to make the paint harden and last longer. These resins were natural juices which could be extracted from some kinds of trees or from insects.

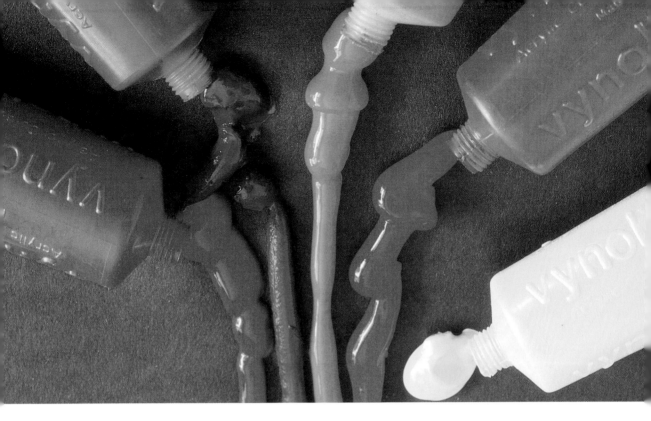

Today, paint is made in factories so that you don't have to grind and mix your own pigments every time you want to paint a picture. Workers mix the pigments with binders and resins to make hundreds of litres of paint at a time. In the paint factory, pigment, binder and water are mixed in a huge tank called a high- speed disperser. Powerful blades spin round and round to spread the pigment evenly through the paint. At this stage, the paint is a paste.

Next the paste flows into smaller tanks where more water and other liquids are added. Afterwards, workers check the paint for quality and colour. Then the paint can be packed so that it's ready for you and your brush.

Factory-made paints come in many bright colours.

FUN TO DO

You can make your own black paint from a natural pigment, charcoal.

FUN TO DO

Charcoal paint

YOU WILL NEED:

a mixing bowl
a small knife
1 piece of charcoal
1 teaspoon of vegetable
   oil
a paintbrush
paper
an egg yolk
1 teaspoon of milk

1. Use the knife to scrape about a teaspoon of powder from the piece of charcoal into the mixing bowl.

2. Mix the powder with the vegetable oil. This is your paint.

3. Paint a small picture on the drawing paper. Make a note of the time when you finish painting.

4. Every hour or so, touch your painting to see if it has dried. Write down how long it takes before it's completely dry.

5. Now try mixing more charcoal powder with different binders. You can use some egg yolk or a teaspoon of milk. Paint a picture with each new paint you make. Time how long it takes for each one to dry and compare the different shades of black.

* **Ask your parents to help you.**

Colours from wax

When you open a box of wax crayons, you have a whole range of bright and pale colours to choose from. You can find the exact blue of the sky and a rich yellow for the sun so that your picture is as bright as the day outside.

You know from their name that your crayons are made from wax, but have you ever stopped to think about the wax? Crayons, candles and polish are all made from a type of wax called paraffin wax. Paraffin wax comes from oil.

Powdered pigments are mixed with hot liquid wax.

Of course, the most important thing about crayons is their colour. Huge amounts of pigments are needed to make the colours. At the crayon factory, paraffin wax is heated until it forms a liquid. Then the powdery pigments are mixed with the wax.

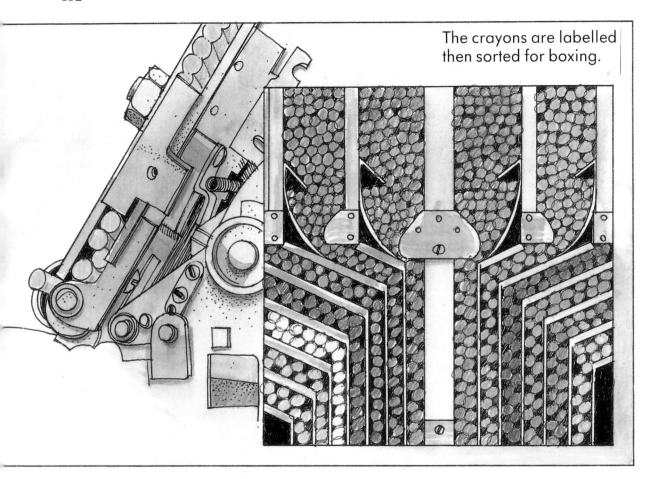

The crayons are labelled then sorted for boxing.

The coloured wax is then poured into hundreds of metal openings, or moulds. When the wax cools and hardens, the crayons are turned out of their moulds.

Next, the crayons are rolled into a machine where each crayon is labelled with a paper wrapper. Lastly, a sorting machine neatly arranges one crayon of each colour into a row. Each row of crayons is slotted into a box.

FUN TO DO

Use your wax crayons to make a new kind of picture.

FUN TO DO

A crayon picture

YOU WILL NEED:

4 or 5 wax crayons, of
    different colours
a piece of paper about 15
    centimetres square
newspaper
a sharp wooden stick (like
    a toothpick)

* Ask your parents to
help you.

1. Cover your table with newspaper so that you don't make a mess.

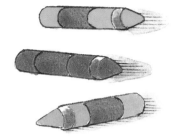

2. Cover your paper with wide stripes of each colour crayon, except for the darkest colour you have.

3. Cover all the stripes with a thick layer of the darkest colour crayon.

4. Use the wooden stick to scratch a picture in the top layer of wax. The colour of the different stripes underneath will show through.

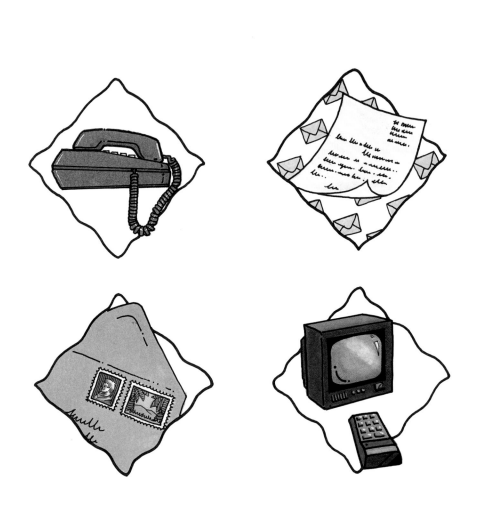

FIND OUT ABOUT

things that keep people in touch

How does a telephone work?
Where does a letter go after it is posted?
When were stamps first used?

Speaking through a wire

The first telephone didn't look or work like the phones we use today. You could speak into it, but you wouldn't hear anyone answer. In other words, the first telephone could only send, or transmit, messages. The American inventor Alexander Graham Bell used it to send the very first telephone message in 1876. He telephoned to his assistant with the instruction — "Mr Watson, come here. I want you!"

The first telephone to be sold was made in the United States of America. It looked like a box with a cup fixed to one end. Later, telephones were attached to the wall and had a cup for speaking and a hand-held receiver for listening. Eventually, telephones were made with a receiver that could be used both for talking and listening.

Today's telephones are still made this way but they have come a long way since Alexander Graham Bell's day. You might use a telephone with a dial or with buttons, and it could be one of many shapes and colours. What happens when you ring up a friend? You can find out by following your message into the telephone.

1. Alexander Graham Bell and the first telephone
2. An old-fashioned Bakelite telephone
3. A modern push-button telephone
4. A modern 'cartoon' telephone

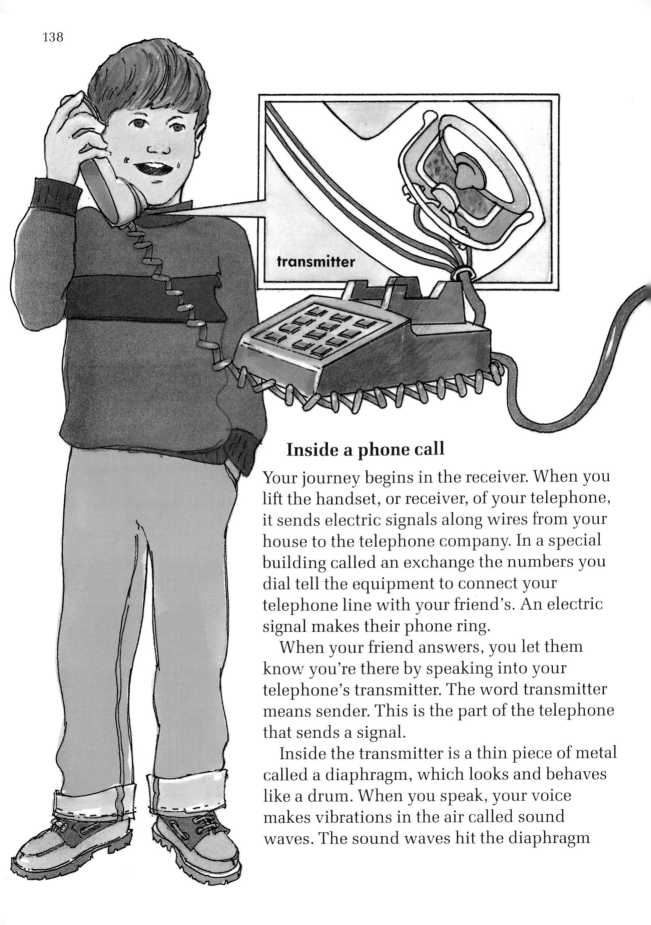

transmitter

Inside a phone call

Your journey begins in the receiver. When you lift the handset, or receiver, of your telephone, it sends electric signals along wires from your house to the telephone company. In a special building called an exchange the numbers you dial tell the equipment to connect your telephone line with your friend's. An electric signal makes their phone ring.

When your friend answers, you let them know you're there by speaking into your telephone's transmitter. The word transmitter means sender. This is the part of the telephone that sends a signal.

Inside the transmitter is a thin piece of metal called a diaphragm, which looks and behaves like a drum. When you speak, your voice makes vibrations in the air called sound waves. The sound waves hit the diaphragm

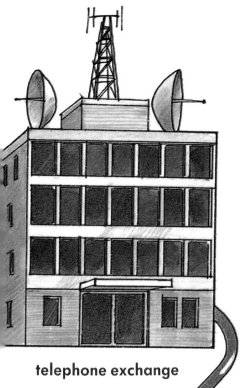

telephone exchange

making it move backwards and forwards to match the sounds of your voice. Then the diaphragm sends a flow, or current, of electricity along wires to your friend's telephone.

When the electricity reaches your friend's receiver, it enters an electromagnet. This is a magnet which works when electricity flows through it. The electromagnet and other magnets set off new sound waves which move another diaphragm. The movement of this diaphragm makes sounds that exactly match your voice. It seems as though it would take forever for your voice to make such a long trip, but it takes less than a second!

Telephones can be used for much more than just calling and talking to people. And they will certainly be able to do even more in the future. Here are some of the amazing things phones can do.

receiver

You can use a fax machine to send words and pictures over the telephone line.

Phones that write and draw

A facsimile, or fax, machine allows you to send words and pictures over telephone lines. You put a page with a message on it into one fax machine and dial the number of the receiving fax machine. Your machine changes the message into electric signals that travel over phone lines from one fax to another. The receiving machine changes the signals back into your message and prints a copy.

Phones for deaf people

A new kind of telephone for deaf people has been invented. It's called a videophone. A tiny video camera and television screen allow deaf people to talk to each other in sign language. The videophone is connected to the ordinary telephone system.

Phones that travel

Cordless telephones allow you to walk round the house and even go out of doors, while you're speaking on the telephone. These telephones have a base that is connected to telephone lines, and a handset, which sends radio signals to the base. Radio signals are electric signals sent through the air.

When you call a friend from a car phone, radio signals are sent to a nearby station that has an aerial. Next, the call goes to a switching station. Finally, it goes to the phone company that sends it to your friend's telephone.

Telephones that talk

Telephones can be connected to a recording machine that can take your calls when you're out, or busy. You record your own voice saying something like, "Hello. Leave a message and I'll call you back." Then the answering machine plays the message and records what your caller says. You play back the caller's message when you come home.

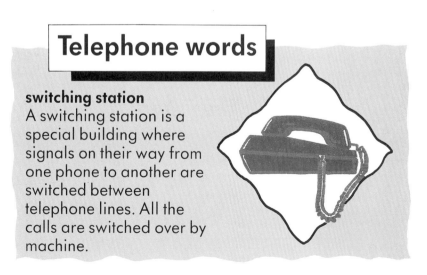

Telephone words

switching station
A switching station is a special building where signals on their way from one phone to another are switched between telephone lines. All the calls are switched over by machine.

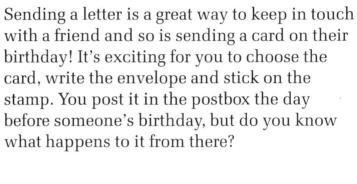

KEEPING IN TOUCH

All the way by post

Sending a letter is a great way to keep in touch with a friend and so is sending a card on their birthday! It's exciting for you to choose the card, write the envelope and stick on the stamp. You post it in the postbox the day before someone's birthday, but do you know what happens to it from there?

In most countries, the post is collected on the same day. The postman drives up in his van. He unlocks the postbox and tips the letters into his mail bag. Then he loads the bag onto his van and drives to the post office in town. At the post office, the local mail is separated from the mail going further away. If your friend lives in another town, the card is sent to the nearest large sorting office.

That evening, at the sorting office, the mail bags are emptied onto a moving belt and carried into a machine that sorts the letters by size. The letters are still jumbled up, back to front and upside-down. The machine turns all the letters the right way round, and then cancels the stamps by printing lines on them. That means the stamps can't be used again.

The letters are sorted by size, turned the right way round and then the stamps are cancelled.

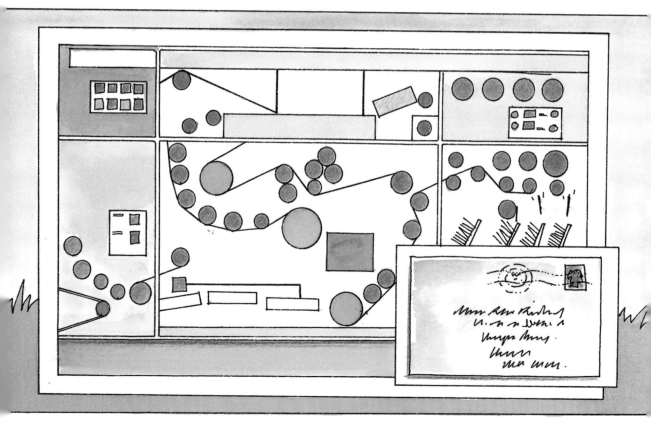

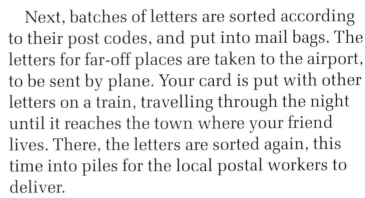

Next, batches of letters are sorted according to their post codes, and put into mail bags. The letters for far-off places are taken to the airport, to be sent by plane. Your card is put with other letters on a train, travelling through the night until it reaches the town where your friend lives. There, the letters are sorted again, this time into piles for the local postal workers to deliver.

In the morning, the postman takes his bag full of letters and sets out on his delivery route. Your card will hopefully reach your friend's house the day after you posted it, just in time to say happy birthday!

Letter words

post code
Many countries have a system of post codes which is used to speed up the delivery of mail. The codes are made up of numbers and letters.

The codes tell the postal workers exactly where the mail should be delivered. Many sorting offices use special machinery which sorts mail by its post code.

The letters are sorted by post code, sent to the right sorting office and delivered to the right address.

FUN TO DO

Make some stickers to stick on the envelopes of your letters.

FUN TO DO

Stickers

YOU WILL NEED:
1 small packet of
   unflavoured gelatine
1 tablespoon cold water
3 tablespoons very hot
   water
½ tablespoon golden
   syrup
a small bowl
a paintbrush
a small, homemade
address labels pictures to
use as stickers
an envelope
a letter you've written

* Ask your parents to
help you.

1. Pour the cold water
into the bowl. Sprinkle the
gelatine over the water.
Watch it wrinkle up. This
will take about 5 minutes.

2. When the gelatine is
soft, add the hot water
and the golden syrup.
Stir until the gelatine
dissolves.

Remember!
Very hot water can burn,
so be careful.

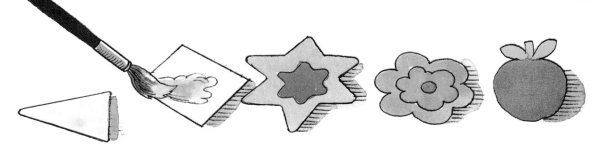

3. Brush the mixture over the backs of your address labels and sticker pictures. Let it dry.

4. When the glue is dry, moisten it by licking the pieces or using a little water. Place the address label in the middle of the envelope. Use the stickers to decorate the letter and seal the envelope flap.

5. Now your letter has a personal touch. Don't forget the stamp!

Stamping It

You will see all sorts of interesting and colourful pictures on postage stamps. Some stamps show birds, fish, plants and animals, while others remind us of famous people, inventors, explorers and sportsmen, or well-known historical events, anniversaries and celebrations. You'll see ships, planes, bicycles and trains. And there are stamps with the head of prime ministers, presidents, kings or queens on them. Just about anything you can think of has been pictured on a postage stamp somewhere in the world!

Stamps are quite a modern invention. They have only existed for about 150 years. Before stamps, people had to ask a letter carrier to deliver their letters and parcels for them. The person who received the letter had to pay for the service. It was so expensive that some people couldn't afford to send letters at all.

In 1840, an English schoolteacher, Rowland Hill, changed all that. He persuaded the government that it would be a good idea to introduce just one standard cost for sending a letter anywhere in Great Britain. He also introduced the first postage stamp, which had to be bought at a post office and stuck on the letter by the sender. The stamp showed that the sender had paid for the delivery and the receiver didn't have to pay anything more.

Stamps around the world

Soon, other countries began to copy the postal system of Great Britain. The first stamps showed the head of Queen Victoria of England. The stamps were known as the penny black and the twopenny blue because of their colours. The name of the country was not printed on the stamp and Great Britain is still the only country in the world that does not put its name on stamps.

The first stamps issued by the United States government showed Benjamin Franklin on the stamp known as the five cent brown and the American president George Washington on the one known as the ten cent black.

Stamps in Australia were first issued in the state of New South Wales on 1 January 1850. The first stamps in the state of Victoria followed two days later.

Early stamps issued by the Cape of Good Hope, in South Africa, were different from the usual stamps — they were a triangular shape. Some of them are now very valuable.

1

2

3

1. Queen Victoria of England
2. Benjamin Franklin of America
3. George Washington of America

Starting a stamp collection

Can you learn about the history of the world by looking at tiny pictures? Yes you can — you can collect stamps. All you need is an album to keep them in and some special tools for handling them carefully.

Save stamps from letters or buy new ones from the post office. To get started, you might buy a few packets of stamps.

You can keep your stamps in a special album. Some albums show stamps grouped by country or by topic. If you prefer, you can make an album out of a scrapbook or notebook.

Use tweezers to handle your stamps to make sure you don't damage them, and use hinges to hold the stamps in place in your album. Hinges are small pieces of paper to which you attach your stamps. This way, you glue your stamps to a hinge instead of to a page in your album, allowing you to move your stamps around.

As your collection grows, you may want other tools, such as a magnifying glass for examining tiny details in your stamps. You can learn more about your stamps from stamp catalogues. The more you know about your stamps, the more fun you can have!

151

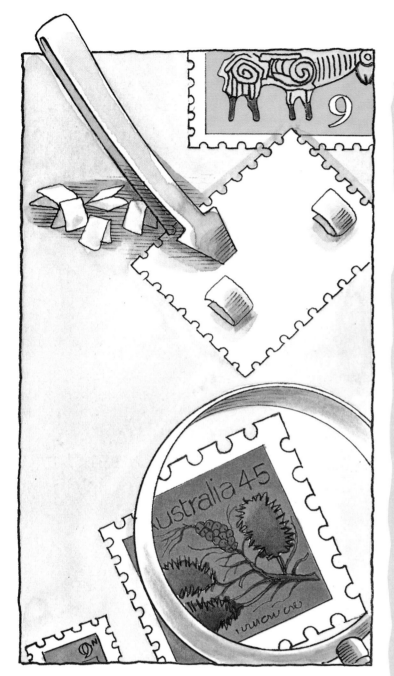

Tweezers and a magnifying glass are useful tools for stamp collectors.

Stamp words

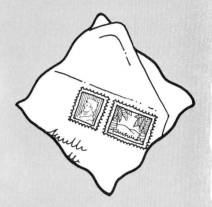

perforation
A perforation is the line of small holes along the edges of stamps. Perforations make it easy for you to tear a stamp off a sheet without using scissors. They were the idea of an Irish engineer named Henry Archer. They were first used in 1854.

philatelist
A philatelist is the name given to a stamp collector. This name comes from two Greek words, philos, which means loving, and atelos, which means paid. A person who collects stamps shows a love of stamps, and stamps are proof that a person has paid to send a letter.

Tuning in

A group of clowns cartwheel down the street. Decorated trucks glide by. Drums roll and trumpets blare as a brass band passes by. It's a parade! But what happens if you can't go to see it? Will you miss it altogether? No! You can keep in touch with all sorts of events by tuning in to a television.

Television words

aerial

An aerial is a kind of wire that receives or sends out radio waves. The word aerial means in the air. Aerials can be lots of different shapes, from the small aerial you have on your house, to the huge broadcast aerials.

microphone

A microphone is an instrument for transmitting sounds. It changes sound into electric signals which can be sent through the air. Microphones can also make quiet sounds louder.

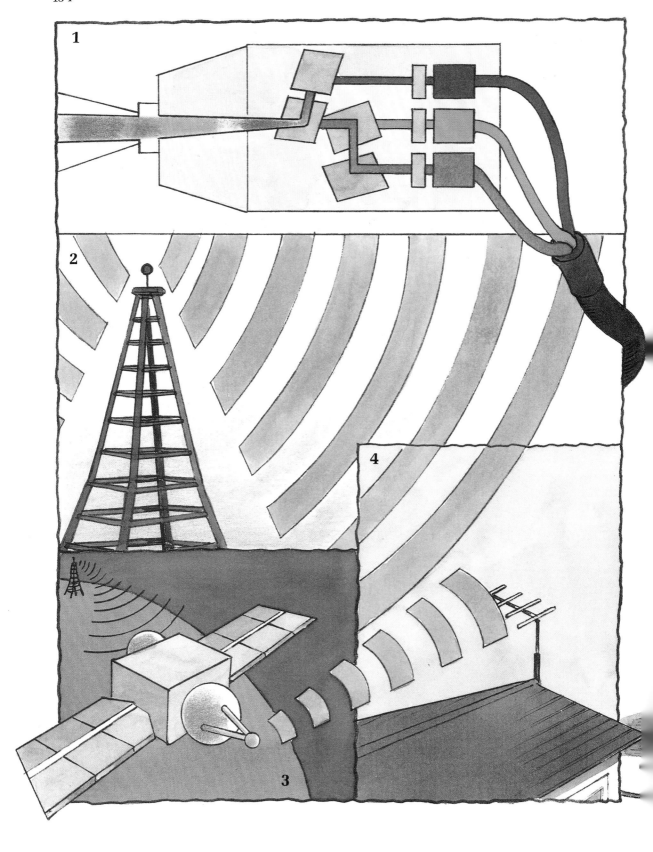

1. The television camera changes the light into electric signals.
2. The electric signals are sent through the air from the broadcast aerial.
3. Satellites in space are used to carry signals over long distances.
4. A television aerial on your house receives the signals and sends them to your TV.

Television cameras and microphones record the parade as it happens. Inside the camera, the lens focuses the light from the scene. Mirrors inside the camera reflect the light and split it into three primary colours — red, green, and blue. All the colours you see on your television screen are made from tiny dots of red, green and blue.

A tube the camera changes the light into electricity. These electric signals will become the pieces of the picture being televised to you.

The electric signals, called waves, travel through the air from a television broadcast aerial. A series of aerials in space,or satellites, can carry signals over long distances.

Your television also has an aerial. It receives the signals and transmits them to the set. Once inside, the speaker and the picture tube turn the electric signals into the sound and light patterns that entered the microphone and the television camera. And the parade marches on, live, before your eyes!

Index

This index is an alphabetical list of the important words and topics in this book.

When you are looking for a special piece of information, you can look for the word in the list and it will tell you which pages to look at.

Acknowledgement

The publishers of **Childcraft** gratefully acknowledge the following artists, photographers and agencies for illustrations used in this volume. All illustrations are the exclusive property of the publishers of Childcraft unless names are marked with an asterix*.

Cover	Tony Kenyon, B.L. Kearley Ltd
6	Kate Davies
8–13	Robert Byrd
14–15	Tony Kenyon, B.L. Kearley Ltd
16–20	Trevor Ridley, B.L. Kearley Ltd
21	Tony Kenyon, B.L. Kearley Ltd
22	The Telegraph Colour Library*
22–23	Linda Birch, B.L. Kearley Ltd
24	Tony Kenyon, B.L. Kearley Ltd
25	Linda Birch, B.L. Kearley Ltd
25–26	Lane Yerkes
26	The Telegraph Colour Library*
27	Tony Kenyon, B.L. Kearley Ltd
28	Lane Yerkes
29	Linda Birch, B.L. Kearley Ltd
30	Lane Yerkes
30–31	Linda Birch, B.L. Kearley Ltd
32–33	Tony Kenyon, B.L. Kearley Ltd
34–35	Mark Peppé, B.L. Kearley Ltd
36	Tony Kenyon, B.L. Kearley Ltd
37	Tony Kenyon, B.L. Kearley Ltd
38–40	Trevor Ridley, B.L. Kearley Ltd
42	Kate Davies
44	Linda Birch, B.L. Kearley Ltd
45	Greg Evans Photo Library*
46–47	Kevin Kimber, Artbeat Artist's Agency
48–49	Tony Kenyon, B.L. Kearley Ltd
50–51	Robert Byrd
51–53	The International Institute for Cotton*
54–55	Mark Peppé, B.L. Kearley Ltd
56–57	Mark Peppé, B.L. Kearley Ltd
58	Tony Kenyon, B.L. Kearley Ltd
59	Robert Byrd
60–61	Mark Peppé, B.L. Kearley Ltd
62–63	Trevor Ridley, B.L. Kearley Ltd
64	Kate Davies
66–67	Tony Kenyon, B.L. Kearly Ltd
68	Trevor Ridley, B.L. Kearley Ltd
70–75	Tony Kenyon, B.L. Kearley Ltd
76	The Telegraph Colour Library*
77	Tony Kenyon, B.L. Kearley Ltd
78–79	Mark Peppé, B.L. Kearley Ltd
80–85	Tony Kenyon, B.L. Kearley Ltd
86	Kate Davies
88–92	Kevin Kimber, Artbeat Artist's Agency
93	Tracy Carrington
93–95	Trevor Ridley, B.L. Kearley Ltd
96–97	Tony Kenyon, B.L. Kearley Ltd
98–99	Trevor Ridley, B.L. Kearley Ltd
99	Tony Kenyon, B.L. Kearley Ltd
100	Berol Limited*
101–103	Tony Kenyon, B.L. Kearley Ltd
104	The Telegraph Colour Library*
104–107	Trevor Ridley, B.L. Kearley Ltd
107	Tony Kenyon, B.L. Kearley Ltd
108–109	Kevin Kimber, Artbeat Artist's Agency
110	Kevin Kimber, Artbeat Artist's Agency
111	Tony Kenyon, B.L. Kearley Ltd
112	Kate Davies
114–115	Kevin Kimber, Artbeat Artist's Agency
116–117	Mark Peppé, B.L. Kearley Ltd
117	Greg Evans Photo Library*
118	Kevin Kimber, Artbeat Artist's Agency
119	Mark Peppé, B.L. Kearley Ltd
120–121	Lisa Hall, Artbeat Artist's Agency
122	Tony Kenyon, B.L. Kearley Ltd
123	Greg Evans Photo Library*
124–125	Mark Peppé, B.L. Kearley Ltd
126–127	Tony Kenyon, B.L. Kearley Ltd
128	Greg Evans Photo Library*
129	Tony Kenyon, B.L. Kearley Ltd
130–131	Lisa Hall, Artbeat Artist's Agency
131–132	Trevor Ridley, B.L. Kearley Ltd
133	Tony Kenyon, B.L. Kearley Ltd
134	Kate Davies
136–137	Mark Peppé, B.L. Kearley Ltd
138–139	Trevor Ridley, B.L. Kearley Ltd
140	Greg Evans Photo Library*
141	Kevin Kimber, Artbeat Artist's Agency
142–145	Trevor Ridley, B.L. Kearley Ltd
146–147	Tony Kenyon, B.L. Kearley Ltd
149	Kevin Kimber, Artbeat Artist's Agency
150	Tracy Carrington
151–155	Tony Kenyon, B.L. Kearley Ltd